And It's All Over . . .

This book is dedicated to my wife Sheila and the thousands of football widows around the world without whose great patience our beloved game would have withered and died. God bless them all.

D.F.

And It's All Over ...
DAVID FRANCEY
with PHIL McENTEE

JOHN DONALD PUBLISHERS LTD
EDINBURGH

With a Scottish managerial legend, Jim McLean, boss of Dundee United, one of the most successful Scottish teams of the 1980s. United narrowly lost the 1987 UEFA Cup Final to Gothenburg of Sweden but the behaviour of their fans was so sportingly exemplary that FIFA made a special award of £20,000 to the club.

Foreword

Football is first and foremost an entertainment. You can call it a sport developed to a high degree of technique over its hundred-odd years of existence by managers and coaches. A tactical battleground for 'insiders'. Or you could say it's a business, as it undoubtedly is for managers whose livelihoods depend on it.

But if football ever loses its capacity to entertain it can shut up shop. At Dundee United I like to think that all the sweat and tears that have been expended over many years have one overriding aim. To win, yes, but to win with some style. We have tried to entertain the paying public.

David Francey was one of the best-known voices on Scottish radio for over thirty years in his capacity as a leading football commentator. As BBC Scotland's number one, his great virtue was that he never lost sight of the fact that folk who were interested in the game deserved to be entertained. He spoke for the many thousands of fans who, for one reason or another, could not be present at the great event. And, for Francey, every football match was an 'event'.

He gave pleasure to millions. He emphasised the positive side of the game. He made it live. He was, indeed, an entertainer. I am pleased to introduce his story.

Jim McLean,
Manager,
Dundee United FC.

© David Francey 1988

All rights reserved. No part of this publication may be reproduced in any form or by any means without the prior permission of the publishers, John Donald Publishers Ltd., 138 St Stephen Street, Edinburgh, EH3 5AA.

ISBN 0 85976 221 1

Filmset by Newtext Composition Ltd., Glasgow
Printed in Great Britain by Bell & Bain Ltd., Glasgow

Introduction

The first time I worked with my co-author Phil McEntee was in Yugoslavia in 1982 when Dundee United were playing Radnicki Nis in a European tie.

It happened to be one of Phil's first broadcasting experiences but his summaries during my live two-hour commentary suggested no nervousness whatsoever.

However, my lasting memory of that evening is of my announcing at the end of the broadcast: 'And so from Nis, here in Yugoslavia, on behalf of Phil McEntee and myself, this is David Francey wishing you all good night.'

The word 'night' had scarcely faded from my lips when I heard Phil's voice, strangely hoarse, say: 'God – I'm away for a double brandy.'

David Francey

Contents

Foreword		v
Introduction		vii
1	Thanks for the Memory	1
2	In a Rut – at 17!	7
3	A Letter to the Beeb	11
4	Summoned to Broadcasting House	15
5	On Trial for Two Guineas	19
6	Keep Them Entertained	27
7	Oh Dear, Oh Dear	33
8	Jock Stein	41
9	A Nice Man	51
10	Midsummer Madness in Argentina	65
11	Surviving in a Tough Business	75
12	Teuchter for a Day	83
13	Who'd Be a Referee?	85
14	Scottish Football's Blackest Day	91
15	The New Firm	93
16	The Principals	103
17	The Future	107
18	And It's All Over!...	115
Index		119

1

Thanks for the Memory

The date was Tuesday, 26th May, 1987. The 41,384 tartan-clad fans on Hampden Park's famous slopes were clearly relishing some superb football even if Andy Roxburgh's Scottish team were faring no better than their predecessors against the sorcery of Brazil. In this, their seventh meeting with the South American magicians, the Scots were still without a win. It was plain to even the most chauvinistic Scot at Hampden that night that that elusive honour could not be obtained at the expense of these colourful and talented visitors.

To me there was no great mystery about this. Every player in those famous canary yellow jerseys was a master of his craft, a complete footballer, an instinctive ball player. One felt that even goalkeeper Carlos could have set off on a mazy upfield foray had the occasion demanded. In truth Scotland did not stretch him too far in his allotted task, but since Carlos elected to remain where he was meant to be, the theory was never put to the test.

Nevertheless I was not surprised to see the Brazilians in total control of the situation, for I had been privileged to see them learn their trade – or the basics of it – at grassroots level.

During Scotland's South American tour in 1977, I watched, fascinated, as crowds of dusky-skinned urchins, most wearing only tattered shorts, displayed incredible ball skills on the fabulous Copacabana Beach in Rio with the blazing sun as their umbrella.

It was an eye opener, an education and a thought provoker. Here, surely, was the way to develop young footballers. Give them a ball and let them get on with practising their skills without the pressure of competition which we foist on our kids from the earliest possible age in this part of the world. There, on a beach, with nothing to gain but the pride in achieving complete mastery of a football, were the future Peles, Rivelinos, Garinchas and Zicos.

Ten years on and they had come back to taunt us again with the excellence of their individual and collective game. The names are new but no less exotic – Geraldao, Ricardo, Muller and, I believe, a future Pele, one Mirandinha. The average age is 22 but those magical skills are already formed on a carpet of sand years ago and 5,000 miles away.

'And as the closing seconds tick away it's Brazil in the lead by two goals to nil. Referee Luis Agnolin, of Italy, is looking at his watch. There goes the final whistle – and it's all over.'

And it's all over. I had used the phrase a thousand times in thirty-five years of broadcasting. On this night I would use it for the last time. David Francey, Radio's voice of Scottish football, had switched off his microphone for good.

But if the commentaries and the football had finished, my evening still held many surprises. BBC Scotland's sports programme 'International Sportsound' suddenly became a vehicle for a host of tributes which left me feeling proud, humble and frankly dazed. Paraphrased they went like this:

Ernie Walker, secretary of the SFA: 'David is a wee bit special. He has been a long time in the business and we are marking this by making a presentation to him. The great thing about David is that having worked in football a long time, he supported football and didn't knock the game. He has never criticised or ridiculed football and we have appreciated his efforts and we are sorry to see him go.'

David Will, president of the SFA: 'What can you say about David Francey? I remember him fondly over the years. I hope you have a super retirement, David.'

Andy Roxburgh, the national coach: 'He has done a wonderful job. We have had some great thrills listening to him. He has been a really exciting voice on the radio and has given great service to the promotion of Scottish football.'

Craig Brown, assistant national coach: 'I think you started my brother Jock off on his career. All the lads in the dressingroom think most highly of you. I have thoroughly enjoyed listening to

Thanks for the Memory

In relaxed mood outside Hampden before the Rous Cup international between Scotland and Brazil in 1987, his last commentary. Brazil were the eventual winners of the competition. Picture courtesy of Frank Tocher, Programme Publications.

you. I can't mimic you but Charlie Nicholas won the David Francey competition in the dressingroom.'

Willie Miller, captain of Scotland: 'I would like to wish David Francey all the best on his retirement. I would hope he has many happy years.'

Brian McClair, Scotland striker: 'I would just like to say to the best commentator in Scottish football, all the best on your retirement.'

Murdo MacLeod, Scotland defender: 'I hope David Francey has a good retirement. He has been great for football over so

Pat Chalmers, Controller of BBC Scotland, expresses the Corporation's best wishes to the commentator on his retirement. Picture courtesy of the BBC.

many years and deserves a very good rest.'

Ally McCoist, Scotland striker: 'All the best on your retirement, David.'

Finally it was the turn of Alex McLeish, Scotland defender. Alex is an inveterate prankster and joker. I have seen many a passenger lounge in an airport in something of an uproar as a result of one of his favourite pranks. As a passenger would hurry past the seat which he and a bunch of his team-mates would be occupying, he would drop a few coins on the floor. Ninety per cent of the time the passing passenger would break stride and hunt around the floor convinced that he had dropped something. I was caught myself, but quickly learned to look for the big red head, and if he was in the vicinity, no matter how innocent he looked, I ignored the jingling coins.

It followed, therefore, that Alex's tribute was something different. Breaking into the David Francey voice he set about describing an incident during a Cowdenbeath v. Alloa match involving ex-team-mate Willie Gardner's father eating a mince pie!

Alex's final words were, however, as always, sincere, 'Good luck to the big man.'

2
In a Rut – at 17!

For the first and only time on that sunny Saturday afternoon in April, 1963, Wembley Stadium was silent and still. Although we were in a decade when doing one's 'own thing' became fashionable, we had not yet been infected with the obscene notion that serious injury to a player is a cause for widespread rejoicing in the opposing camp.

At that moment, one hundred thousand pairs of eyes were riveted on turf that was hallowed, manicured and still the envy of the world, though somehow dangerous. More precisely, the undivided attention of the 100,000 was homed in on the prostrate figure in the dark blue of Scotland who was very obviously in agony.

Ambulance men were summoned urgently. There followed the long stretcher ride to the dressing room to the muted accompaniment of sympathetic handclapping from Englishmen and Scots alike. A broken limb knows no boundaries of race.

We did not know it at the time but the footballing career of Eric Caldow, Rangers' and Scotland's gifted left back, would never reach such exalted heights again.

It was a personal tragedy for him, and Eric had the nation's sympathy on that bittersweet day for Scotland and indeed afterwards. And later, when time repaired the hurt, he had the consolation of memories of life at the top of his profession, of great games won and lost, of honours gained, of recognition.

Compare Caldow's case with that of David Francey, a teenager nursing a youngster's dream of a career as a professional footballer. What lad who has kicked a ball has not entertained such fantasies, however fleetingly?

Besides, there was the hint of some substance to this young

David's verdict: Eric Caldow played football much better than he plays the piano! Picture by Alan Ewing.

man's hopes. There was some promise there. He had played for his school, Hyndland Senior Secondary, at every age level. Now, at 17, he was a regular with Western Amateurs FC.

Junior scouts had been taking careful note of his goalscoring prowess. And forty-odd years ago, the junior game was a much more common route to senior football than it is now.

At any rate, the youngster I was, was happy with life and his football until a black and dismal Glasgow afternoon put paid to his dreams. For Wembley, substitute a Glasgow Corporation park. Instead of an audience of a hundred thousand the cast comprised two trainers with sopping wet sponges, five muddy kids looking on, one clutching a tanner ba', two enthusiastic teams and, incongruously, tethered behind our goal, the goalie's black and white mongrel.

In the split second between my brain reading the pass and ordering my body into a reverse turn, it happened. The bumpy, rutted, cruel pitch dealt me a sickening blow. The right foot —

which had earlier hammered in three goals – did not turn, wedged as it was in a water-filled and concealed pothole.

The result was excruciating. The right ankle stubbornly defied the almighty, gravity-aided jerk. The knee joint succumbed. Weeks later the probing fingers and sorrowfully shaking head of the then Rangers trainer Arthur Dixon said it all. Clubs who had been showing an interest in this promising boy would look no more.

Medical opinion was also quite definite. 'You have a perfectly good knee for leading an ordinary life and going about your everyday business,' said the doctor. 'But if you persist in playing football you will end up with a permanent limp.'

It had to be said. But it was a crushing verdict to deliver to an eager 17-year-old. The embryonic footballing career of David Francey, an aspiring inside forward who played deep – or, in today's parlance, behind the main strikers – was at an end.

Hyndland Senior Secondary School and Western Amateurs had seen the best of me. Indeed all anyone would ever see of me kicking a ball.

In truth, I thought the world was at an end, too.

3
A Letter to the Beeb

How is it then that, having been written off footballwise at a tender age, I have managed to enjoy for thirty-five years now a career in what is for me the greatest game in the world?

Why have I been privileged to commentate on some of the greatest games affecting Scotland and Scottish teams over the past twenty-odd years through the marvellous and exciting medium of radio?

Was it fate? The gift of the gab? The luck to have been born with a voice that lent itself fairly readily to training in singing and projection and, therefore, was suited to this voracious medium? Was it love of the game? Or simply an ability to impart the drama and excitement intrinsic to the game of football in a lively and entertaining way to the listening audience? A bit of each, I suspect.

Looking back, if fate, in the shape of a Glasgow pothole hadn't cut short my hopes of a football career, a certain Mr Hitler would probably have done so anyway. At any rate, my life, like that of millions of others in the early 1940s, was forced to take an unscheduled turn.

But long before that the seeds of a lifelong love affair with football had been planted and nurtured in fertile soil.

To begin at the beginning, as Dickens once said, I was born in 1924 in the Partick district of Glasgow. We were a sizeable tribe and David Maxwell Francey was the youngest of four boys and four girls in a family with fairly wide-ranging interests.

My oldest brother Bill was and is a very good musician and Jim, the second oldest, was a good footballer in his youth. Both these older lads emigrated to America when I was still fairly young.

This meant I was probably closer to John, the next boy to

me. John is the artist of the family, keen on painting and writing. He still lives in Erskine.

If we weren't exactly a silver spoon family, we were hardly uncomfortable. Dad worked as an engineer in the Glasgow shipyards and, if I wasn't born with a silver spoon in my mouth, God certainly gave me a tongue in my head, or perhaps an inherited touch of the blarney.

My father Tom Francey was an Irishman, from Ballymena, who had come over to Glasgow from Ulster with his young bride Agnes not only to help ensure that Clyde-built meant the best there was then in shipbuilding but to spread the good news of the gospel.

He was in his spare time an evangelistic preacher of the Plymouth Brethren and I remember him as a very fine speaker who could keep a church congregation riveted with the intensity and eloquence of his message. Perhaps some of the Francey ability to communicate came down to me through the genes.

When I was still a toddler, the family moved to the then new suburb of Knightswood on the western fringes of the city and it was there that football got me into my first and – I'm glad to say – so far only spot of bother with the law. Several of us football-daft kids were hauled into juvenile court for the heinous crime of playing football in the street!

Enter my father and his persuasive ways. He appeared in court to argue on my behalf, pointing out to the law what a good boy I was. He made such a fine impression that the police inspector who took the court sent me on my way with only a warning and the admonition: 'I don't ever want to see you here again.'

He didn't, though I'm not so sure his words were a deterrent. In retrospect, our transgressions with a tanner rubber ba' were mild in comparison to the problems of modern urban delinquency. But in the 1930s respect for authority was almost absolute.

If memory serves right, we seemed to play football morning, noon and night in those days and so we continued to 'sin' in that respect. We must have been a perfect pest to the good

A Letter to the Beeb

Meeting an old friend and legend. Francey with Willie Thornton, whose debut for Rangers he saw in 1936. Photo Alan Ewing.

folk of Knightswood struggling to keep their gardens tidy and free of wee boys retrieving their tanner ba's from among the rosebeds.

I'll never forget dad's performance in court that day. It strikes me now that had he studied law instead of engineering he might well have become an outstanding advocate. Be that as it may, there seemed only one outlet for the energies of his youngest son and that lay in football.

When I wasn't playing the game I was reading about it. In those far-off days, before instant information was available at the touch of a teletext switch, the newspapers were the eagerly awaited supplement to many a lad's boyish fantasies. The sports pages were compulsory reading. Where else to assuage the hunger for news of Saturday's heroes?

The evening papers – and there were three in Glasgow alone – carried on Friday nights the team lists for Saturday's games and I read them and memorised them like a catechism. I can still reel off many of the teams of that era. Then it was just fun. Now I realise that it was, perhaps, a discipline in memory, learned young, that helped cope in later years with the time-consuming but necessary chore of research or 'homework' before each broadcast.

Now I know it is not necessary to be a hen to enjoy a good plate of scrambled eggs. So although it took many years to achieve, I eventually found myself with a football career that has brought the exhilaration, thrills, camaraderie, disappointments and heartbreaks of this great game.

One day in the early 1950s I sat down and wrote a letter. It would prove to be the most important missive I ever penned. It changed my life.

4
Summoned to Broadcasting House

Ten years had passed since Arthur Dixon had signified the end of an aspiring playing career. They had been ten eventful years for David Francey and not wholly without incident for the rest of the world.

I had left Hyndland Senior Secondary School, formal education completed, and taken a job with an insurance company. By now the Second World War was upon us and, although my football injury prevented me initially from being accepted when I volunteered for pilot training in the RAF, I was eventually called up and sent back to 'school' to be equipped as a pilot-navigator.

I hadn't finished my course by the time the Germans were about to pack it in so I never did get into the air. But at this juncture fate gave me a wee push in a direction that undoubtedly helped me get on the air some time later.

During my service abroad with the RAF a friend suggested that my singing voice might be worth developing. I had never given much thought to the possibility of a singing career although I did sing at several camp concerts during the early days of our occupation of Germany.

For thousands of young folk in uniform in camps far away from home the tedium and loneliness of occupation duty posed almost as big a psychological problem for the authorities to cope with as the recently experienced dangers of combat. The top brass in all the services, anxious to keep morale high as the troops waited for the blessed day of demob, encouraged the organisation of these camp concerts, and anyone with any talent at all was roped in to contribute to the general good.

Maybe I could carry this singing business into civvy street? At any rate the day of my release eventually arrived and Corporal David Francey left the RAF with demob suit and pay and some generally unclarified notions about his future.

I remember I had a course of voice production lessons aimed at improving my singing voice, officially listed as 'baritone.' I think they cost me around three guineas a quarter, a lot of money at the time, and certainly more than I forked out for training to develop my speaking voice, around £1 a lesson, and I had about a dozen of these all told.

Money well spent as things were to turn out.

Was the germ of an idea already forming in my mind?

I speak now of 1952. The years AP (After the Pothole) had also gifted me a devoted and understanding wife, a job in the civil service and a baby son, in that order of chronology.

Whatever the economic uncertainties of the 1980s, in 1952 a safe job 'for the Government' with a pension to be anticipated was quite a catch. What it was not was lucrative.

My wife Sheila and I, happily settled in our rented flat in Glasgow's Kelvindale, managed — for a time. When son Michael arrived that year to make three, the Francey resources, frankly, were stretched. A part-time job, which in those more formal times could only be undertaken if it were in keeping with the status of a civil servant, seemed the answer.

The old passion for football had never waned. The spoken and written word, and a feeling for the English language that lingered from schooldays, held their fascination for me. Where else but within the hallowed walls of the BBC's Broadcasting House could both interests be profitably merged?

I sat down to write my letter of application to the BBC.

It was like writing a letter to Santa Claus. I didn't really expect to get what I was asking for. I was hopeful rather than optimistic, and besides, my application was rather vague. I pointed out that I had been considered pretty good at English at school, had had voice training and was football mad. In the circumstances, I asked, had the BBC any job they would consider me able to do?

Sheila, I recall, thought I was mad, or presumptuous, even to ask.

Newlyweds. A wartime picture of David on leave with wife Sheila.

Both of us, then, were pleasantly surprised when, a few days later, an acknowledgement arrived from the personnel manager at the BBC informing me that my application had been forwarded to Mr Peter Thomson, Head of Sport, who would be in touch with me in the near future.

Two weeks later, the glorious summons arrived. A letter, signed with a name known to me as belonging to that outstanding and legendary football commentator, ended simply: 'I should, therefore, be pleased if you would call at Broadcasting House for an audition.' Joy, pride and terror fought for supremacy within me as I prepared mentally for my change of life.

5
On Trial for Two Guineas

Today radio and television studios are as public as railway station superloos. In 1952 they still had an aura of exclusivity about them, and before my audition I had never been closer to a radio studio than a walk through the Botanic Gardens, whose spacious acreage flanks Broadcasting House in Glasgow. It was therefore with some trepidation that I was led by a uniformed commissionaire who, I remember, possessed a voice like that of the late Richard Burton, to the 'Sportsreel' studio.

My first surprise as I shook the proffered hand was that Peter Thomson, of the booming authoritative voice, was a small man. My 6ft 3inch frame towered above him. My next surprise was that this man, the founder of sports broadcasting as we know it in Scotland and who, were he still alive and in the forefront of his profession, would, in today's terms be a superstar, was mild, friendly and abundantly helpful.

Never in our long association was I given cause to alter my first impression of this friendly Fifer. You always knew where you stood with Peter. I thought so highly of him that I could never imagine him doing any wrong. And apart from being a fine man he was a great professional broadcaster.

The audition itself is a largely forgotten blur of script reading, discussion and an extemporaneous report on a recent match I had attended, all done in the terrifying presence of a large metal contraption which seemed to grow out of the middle of the baize-covered table at which the great man and I sat. My future familiarity with lapel microphones was still a long way off.

The upshot of it all was a six-week trial which has lasted for over thirty years. In that time great footballers and lesser ones have come and gone, the Baxters, the Laws, the Johnstones, the Greaves's, the Matthews's, the Eusebios and the Peles. Thirty years is too long on the playing field. But with luck, health and support, a commentator may survive that long.

My understanding as an avid listener was that the owners of the voices one heard on radio drove Rolls Royces. Perhaps those making their way up the ladder had to make do with a Mercedes. Now that I possessed a 'radio voice' I discovered that my weekly fee of two guineas would not stretch that far. Another discovery. Those famous voices belonged to public relations men, journalists, teachers, accountants, actors, civil servants. They, too, had broadcasting voices. All were impassioned sportsmen. Not one had a Rolls Royce.

The Number 2 Corporation bus which took me to Hampden to report my first game clearly had suspension problems. How else to explain the powerful waves of nausea which engulfed me throughout that half-hour journey? There were no such problems on the return trip. Rather, near panic as the bus approached Botanic Gardens and I continued the hunt for inspiration from copious notes.

Not that I had been thrown in at the deep end – or the top – with a great international occasion to report on from our national stadium. But even the prescribed 45 seconds of air time can seem an eternity in which to describe a goalless draw between Queens Park and Arbroath. I suspect my fluency has improved somewhat in the interval, for thirty-odd years later Don Morrison was to write in the *Sunday Mail*: 'The BBC are delighted at the way John Greig interrupts David Francey. This is no mean task!'

Football broadcasters are divided into reporters and commentators. Broadly, reporters describe the game after it has been played. Commentators outline the action as it is happening. As a fledgling reporter, I eagerly awaited the Thursday morning phone call from the sports department secretaries, Luella or Margaret Munro or Liz Rennie, assigning the Saturday game.

Sometimes, though rarely, it was a mediocre First Division game. Usually it was the Second Division. I saw a lot of Stirling

Albion in those days. You see, Stirling were too good for the Second Division and not quite good enough for the First.

Promotion and relegation were thus regular bedfellows and I was a regular visitor.

Visits to Stirling certainly kept one fit. Let me explain. Today it is the simplest of matters for a radio reporter to telephone his report direct from the football ground where he is working to the studio. In the early 'fifties that just wasn't on. A special line was only installed to a ground on great and rare occasions.

Consequently, on a normal Saturday the BBC reporters, scattered throughout Scotland, had to make their way 'on the whistle' to the nearest studio, be it in Glasgow, Edinburgh, Aberdeen or Dundee. Since few of us owned a car in those days, let alone a Rolls Royce, that meant a dash for a train, bus or taxi.

Now in normal circumstances, with a 3pm kick off, there would be no problem in reaching the railway station some half a mile distant from Annfield Park in Stirling. But circumstances at Stirling were not quite normal.

Mr Stirling Albion, alias Tam Ferguson, the club's autocratic chairman, was one of Scottish football's greatest characters. Mr Ferguson, a wealthy coal merchant, did not so much own Stirling Albion. He *was* Stirling Albion. A figure of great authority, he stomped about with a club-like walking stick which was his constant companion. Loved he might have been. Feared he certainly was. Rumours abound in this business, and one that was given much credence was that Tam Ferguson was addressed as 'Sir' by all who met him — his mother included. Rumour also had it that Tam would not have shirked from pulling on a jersey and playing for Albion but for one factor. Not that he was 58 years of age, as he was when I first met him, but that he had an artificial leg.

At any rate, this formidable man had an eye to business. Since the pubs closed at 3pm and since he shared his clientele with the taverns of the town, he would accommodate his patrons. To ensure that the fans could down their pints at leisure and enjoy an unhurried walk and belch on the way to Annfield, Tam decreed that all Albion's home games should kick off at 3.15.

The BBC commentary team at the 1987 Scottish Cup Final. David is flanked by former Rangers manager John Greig and former Celtic striker Brian McClair, now with Manchester United.

As a result, the unfortunate reporter sent to Stirling winced at every robust tackle lest injury time would make the lung bursting dash to the station of no avail. To my credit I only once failed to reach the studio in time with my report. Having boarded the train at Stirling with a full two minutes to spare, I sat down drenched with that feeling of 'happiness is'. I soon drowned in despair as the locomotive, gasping steam, sat in the tunnel outside Glasgow's Queen Street Station for a full half hour.

I dashed to the taxi rank when the train finally pulled in and arrived at Queen Margaret Drive just as the entire 'Sportsreel' team was leaving. Andy Cowan-Martin, who did the Second Division round-up in those days, said: 'It's all over.' It's a phrase I've adopted and used regularly in broadcasts since, but at the time it sounded like the pronouncement of a judge on a condemned man.

In my innocence I believed the whole world would know that Francey had failed in his given assignment. In fact, the damage to the programme, if any, was minimal. Andy had culled the details of my game from an evening newspaper and the listeners were none the wiser that these should have been read, not by him, but by a frustrated reporter who at that moment was sitting in a blacked-out train cursing the vagaries of British Railways' scheduling.

It was simply a hazard of the trade in those days. Looking back, I suppose by today's high-tech standards we were fairly primitive. And yet the show went on. A good show it was, too, and great fun. In those days before television and the spread of commercial radio, 'Sportsreel' was compulsive listening for sports fans, the Saturday evening compendium that fleshed out the bones of the half-hour commentary from the big game which was then all that was normally allotted to Saturday afternoon football.

I suppose it is difficult to be objective about a programme of which one was a part for so long. Certainly sports broadcasting has evolved and moved into other areas to keep pace with a rapidly changing society and its need to 'know'. Instant interviews with leading sports personalities still wet with the sweat of battle, argument and controversy, all play a bigger part in today's broadcasting scene than before.

Despite this, within its time and context, BBC Radio Scotland's 'Sportsreel' was a very fine programme, incorporating news and comment on the entire Scottish sports scene of the day and featuring first-rate broadcasters like Peter Thomson, Robert Dunnet, Andy Cowan-Martin and George Davidson, all household names in their day.

Thomson had his critics and sometimes they were quite cruel. I remember one writer in the early days of television sport commenting: 'Peter Thomson has to look at a script before he can say good evening.'

It was an exaggeration, of course, but it has to be remembered that in those days there were no such things as cue cards. Everything had to be read from a piece of paper on the desk in front of the presenter. There was no board held in front of him at eye level from which he could read the script. To those of us who knew Peter as the fine professional he was, such jibes were nonsense.

There certainly were greater difficulties for the broadcasters in the early days, and the advent of TV brought its own horrors. Although it was a sensational novelty for folk to have a living picture in their homes, the technology was crude by today's standards.

Consequently, recorded highlights of football matches looked erratic, jumpy and often downright amateurish and there was simply nothing the commentator could do about it. A story from one of my early television commentaries illustrates the point.

The cameras were covering a match between Hibs and Motherwell in the days when a game like that still attracted big crowds. The drill was that we had two cameras, a sound camera and a mute camera and only sufficient film in each for a short time.

A crucial incident arrived at exactly the wrong time. Joe Baker, Hibs' skilful and prolific centre forward, went racing into the Motherwell penalty area and, just as he brought his foot back to shoot, John Martis, the somewhat physical and uncompromising Motherwell defender of the era, hit him with a crunching tackle. Joe did about three somersaults in the air, the Hibs supporters screamed 'Penalty' and the Motherwell fans gave Martis a standing ovation.

Unfortunately for the BBC and my commentary, at that precise moment the lead cameraman calmly informed me: 'The film's run out in the sound camera, we'll have to change to the mute.' Horror of horrors, the film in the second camera jammed. By the time we got the confounded thing rolling again, Baker had had the kiss of life, Martis had wiped the blood off his boots, the penalty had been taken and all we obtained on film of this human drama was the sight of the ball hitting the inside of the post and going into the net.

Aha, but we were prepared for just such an eventuality, which was not at all an unusual occurrence at that time. The trick was to get back to the studio and dig out an appropriate crowd scene to fill in the precious space between the 'crime' and the dénouement. Alas, we were totally out of luck that day. The only 'crowd' picture we could lay our hands on was one of three big Teuchters standing with umbrellas and raincoats down to their ankles watching a shinty match!

As if to underline the artificiality of it all, we had the sound of a great roaring crowd dubbed over the scene. I don't know how many people it fooled, but certainly no one who was at Motherwell that day.

It still sometimes amuses me to hear household names in television make the excuse when things go wrong that this is simply an unavoidable hazard of live broadcasting. 'What do you expect in the circumstances?' they ask. In radio we're used to hardly anything else but live broadcasts and, as a result, we have to live with our mistakes.

The truth is I was never really a TV performer. I preferred the radio broadcast right from the start. In radio I believe the commentator is in charge and the sole link between a blind audience and what is happening on the field. In television, the camera is the eye, the boss if you like, and the commentator only has to supplement with fewer words what the viewer can already see.

At any rate, after a spell 'on the telly' I asked Peter Thomson if I could concentrate in the future on radio broadcasting. He was reluctant to agree and told me that he had to use his resources to the best possible advantage. However, my case was helped by the arrival on the scene around that time of a young man whose ambitions lay in the TV medium and who was good at the job. His name – Archie McPherson. So in the end Peter agreed to my suggestion. I was no loss to television. My commentaries on the box were no more than adequate, whereas I like to think some of my radio broadcasts have been, perhaps, a bit more than that. Who knows what would have happened had I persevered with television? I only know I've never regretted my decision to opt for radio completely.

But all this was years after Tam Ferguson and Stirling Albion. The apprentice years were long and hard and enjoyable too, but they passed. The big time was on its way.

Two of the best known names in Scottish sports broadcasting. David with BBC television's Archie McPherson. Photo Alan Ewing.

'I'd like you to record a commentary, David, I think you've got the voice for it,' said Peter one day. If Peter Thomson thought so, who was I to argue? As we listened to the recording, the verdict 'very promising' came as the most exciting words I had heard in years.

I recall telephoning Sheila from an empty office in the BBC with the cryptic command 'Listen'. I was holding the telephone to the tape recorder. The door opened. Peter Thomson stood there. My embarrassment must have been obvious.

'That's all right,' he said. 'Let her hear it. It's worth listening to.'

I was no longer a reporter. I was now a commentator and the year was 1964.

6

Keep Them Entertained

The nearest approach to actually playing football is to provide commentary on it. Radio commentary that is. The commentator is involved with every move, every ball kicked. Every action on the field, and many off it, require conversion into word pictures that are picked up and understood by the listener. In that sense, the commentator is all-powerful.

'See that yin Francey,' a Celtic supporter was reported to me as saying, 'he makes your heart stop when Rangers get a shy.'

That marvellous player for Airdrie, Rangers and Scotland, Ian

At a function in Edinburgh with, among others, a young John Greig and Alex Ferguson and former Hearts stars Gordon Marshall and Alan Anderson. Picture courtesy of the Edinburgh *Evening News*.

McMillan, once told me he had latterly refused to allow his late father to listen to my commentaries. 'His heart isn't strong enough to take the excitement,' he said.

I took this as a compliment. While I had no wish to do harm to Mr McMillan's health, or to anyone else's for that matter, football is part of show business and show business is, or should be, about colour and excitement. A football commentary, therefore, should mirror that excitement.

One of the earliest decisions a commentator must make concerns the style he will adopt. Whether he will set out to entertain the listeners or relate flatly what is taking place on the field of play. Rightly or wrongly, my policy from the start has been to try to entertain.

Lest I be misunderstood, let me elaborate. A football commentary may last up to two hours should extra time be played. Indeed, now that certain play-to-the-finish games are decided by penalty kicks, a commentary may exceed two hours. This is a very long time to hold a listener's attention on radio.

Television is another matter. There the pictures are the more important element in the broadcast. It is a known fact that some viewers are content to the point of bliss watching pictures of chimpanzees drinking tea.

The radio listener is more discerning or, perhaps, more quickly bored. Can it be wrong, therefore, to try to hold his attention by injecting an element of excitement into the description which others, watching the action, might not feel?

Is it wrong for 'a very good shot' to become 'A TREMENDOUS DRIVE'? A header described as 'missing the goal by 12 inches' is more likely to bring a listener's ear nearer the tranny if he hears the words '... THERE GOES THE HEADER ... AND IT'S JUST INCHES WIDE OF THAT LEFT HAND POST ...'

I'm aware of a strong preference in the broadcasting world south of the border for the mechanical commentary punctuated by so-called colour. This, it is said, is added largely to accommodate the 'marginal' listener. That may work in England. But I contend that in Scotland when you are talking

Keep Them Entertained

Not the real thing but Francey still enjoys commentating on a game of table football between the players and the Press with Miss Scotland as referee. The microphone, incidentally, is a wine glass.

about football there are no marginal listeners. Up here you either love the game or you're not interested. And if you're a football fan you're tuned in to hear about the action on the field.

Long pauses in commentary during which the speaker informs the listeners of the number of caps a player has won, the fact that he scored in the Cup Final of two years ago and that his uncle is in the Grenadier Guards, serve only to frustrate the listener, especially with the crowd roaring into the effects microphone.

Such interjections are acceptable only if used judiciously and sparingly, preferably when the play has stopped temporarily for some reason or other. There are usually enough of these 'natural breaks' to allow injections of real colour, a description of the crowd, the flags and banners, the singing, the sunshine – or the rain.

I'll give you an example of the kind of 'colour' which I believe

Billy McNeill and Celtic striker Joe Miller win Scottish Brewers Manager and Player of the Month awards at Christmas 1987 and Francey is there to see the Santas, played by Steve Chalmers, on the left, and Ronnie Simpson, right, present the awards. Picture Courtesy John Morgan Associates.

would just not work in Scotland. I was invited down to London by the BBC bosses before setting off to the 1974 World Cup finals in West Germany. The summons had been sent from headquarters to discuss my role in the finals and what would be expected of me in broadcasting terms.

A recording of the FA Cup Final of that year in which Liverpool beat Newcastle United 3-0 was played to demonstrate to me how a football match commentary could be given an extra dimension by the addition of a pithy phrase from time to time. One of my English radio colleagues, Peter Jones, was waxing lyrical about Liverpool's achievements, and in truth Peter is a superb exponent of the technique.

One phrase he used towards the end of the match stuck in my mind. Said Peter: 'It looks now as though the FA Cup will be sailing up the Mersey.'

Now in terms of English listeners that was possibly a fine play on words. But to try to relate that to the Scottish scene would be impossible. How could I possibly say to my listeners:

Keep Them Entertained

'It looks now as though the Scottish Cup will be sailing up the Clyde.' That would sound plain daft.

Someone is alleged to have said that Scottish football writers are supporters with typewriters. I believe the commentators preferred by the fans are punters with microphones.

And if, having picked up brickbats along the way – 'The Francey Frenzy' (*Scottish Field*) or 'The most hysterical voice ever to assault the airwaves' (Gordon Blair, *Sunday Mail*) – there have been more appreciative comments that have come my way in abundance over the years to reinforce the notion that the effort to entertain is the best policy for a commentator.

One of the compliments which has pleased me most is being described at the 1987 Scottish Professional Footballers' Association dinner by the secretary of the PFA, Tony Higgins, as 'the players' commentator.'

7
Oh Dear, Oh Dear

I believe Humphrey Bogart never really did say 'Play it again, Sam.' But why knock a good thing? If imitators wanted a pat phrase with which to give their impression of that famous gravelly voice – and millions did – why should he worry? After all, imitation, they say, is the sincerest form of flattery.

In all modesty I think I can claim I've had a few imitators in my time too, not by any means as many as the famous Bogart, but then I didn't even have a bit part in *Casablanca*! Still, it's a perfectly true story that I was once an also-ran in a David Francey impersonation contest. It happened about six years ago when some of my colleagues organised a fun night at the BBC Club in Glasgow.

Part of the proceedings was a competition to see who could give the best impression of Francey in full flow in a football commentary. I was roped in, too, to submit a tape with half a dozen others or judging. My 'entry', the only true recording, came fourth, which either says something about the 'ear' of the judges or confirms the theory that even familiar sights, sounds or mannerisms become more enjoyable in the take off with a little embellishment. As I recall, the contestants who 'beat' me in the competition exaggerated some of my normal exaggerations of scale and tone. It was terrific fun listening to other people's versions of how one sounds on the air waves.

But then the whole idea of sport and broadcasting, that it should be fun, takes me back to my original assertion that football commentators, or rugby, swimming or tennis ones for that matter, should try to entertain. Sometimes the entertainment is turned back on oneself but maybe that's no bad thing, for the last thing a broadcaster should be is aloof, pompous or given to the ivory-tower mentality.

Now somewhere on some foreign field perhaps, I must have uttered for the consumption of the listeners the immortal words 'Oh dear, Oh dear.' Perhaps they slipped out in a moment of genuine distress over the travail of Scotland or a Scottish club, but the words have stuck to me. Now I don't mind in the least becoming heir to a catchphrase. I only wish I remembered from where the catchphrase came but I can't. Oh dear.

One could have a more dramatic trademark. Yet perhaps mine was an unconscious cry from the heart that we live in an imperfect world. That things are not always as we would wish them to be. That the banana skin lurks just around the corner of our unwariness. I've slipped on a few of those, too, in my time and lived to speak again.

The commentator lives in constant fear of the gaffe, the hastily spoken comment in the heat of the moment that is well meant at the time but inspires nothing but hysterical laughter on the part of the listener or viewer.

David Coleman, one of the great television commentators, was full of excitable good intent during a riveting race in the Montreal Olympics in 1976 when he informed his audience that Jaunterino, the great Cuban runner, had 'opened his legs and showed his class'. David intended no *double entendre* but he had to live with that howler for a long time.

My pal, and colleague at the BBC, John Greig, the former Rangers captain and manager, took some stick as well for his comment during his summarising of the 1986 Skol Cup final at Hampden. Near the end of the match Celtic brought on a substitute in an attempt to swing fortune in their direction. John observed that this was a good move as 'it gives Davie Hay a fresh pair of legs up his sleeve'.

The satirical magazine *Private Eye* picked me up for informing listeners that a certain player had '13 caps under his belt.'

In fairness to David, John and myself there was no real inaccuracy in these statements. With hindsight all three circumstances might have been better expressed, but hindsight is a luxury the broadcaster does not enjoy. The words have to come out quickly since air time is precious, and the one thing radio listeners, or TV viewers, will not tolerate is a stony silence from people regarded by them as experts in their particular field. Therefore, the comments have to be both right and appropriate. This is no simple task, but ninety-nine times out of a hundred they are. The odd howler only serves to illustrate this, as it sticks out like a sore thumb.

However, as to the legend that has grown that I once inadvertently swore during a football broadcast, I must say a vehement 'not guilty'. The fact is I do not swear. This doesn't necessarily make me a better man than the fellow sitting next to me on a train who, for all I know, may have a terrific line in colourful language.

It is simply a fact that, I believe, in my own case is an advantage for both practical and aesthetic reasons. In the first place I have a lot of respect for the English language and believe it has sufficient width and scope to allow us to express ourselves clearly and meaningfully without resorting to the old Anglo-Saxon epithets. Secondly, I know a lot of broadcasters whose language off-duty would make a trooper blush. It always amazes me that they manage to restrain themselves from swearing when they're addressing the nation for, like many other dubious practices, cursing is habit-forming.

The incident in which I am alleged to have sworn on the air concerned Kenny Dalglish, and Kenny has asked me about it more than once. I'm always able to refute the charge. The story goes that during one international my description of a certain incident went something like this: 'And Kenny Dalglish has turned away from his marker – Oh a tremendous piece of control by Dalglish. He's just outside the Spanish penalty area – He's lining up for a shot – there it goes – Oh dear, he's hit the f-----g bar!' Take it from me, I didn't say it. How the story started I just couldn't say.

One other 'gaffe' I'm alleged to have made owes something to the fertile mind of the well-known sports writer and broadcaster Ian Archer with whom I've worked on many occasions.

Ian was summarising for me – that is supplying analysis in

tandem with my commentary – in a Scotland v Rumania game at Hampden some years back. We had both barely had time to settle into our seats in the commentary box – I believe my stopwatch showed only 30 seconds had elapsed since kick off – when the ball was nestling in the back of the Scottish net. I immediately turned to Ian and asked: 'Who scored?' He replied: 'Blowed if I know.'

However, I'm alleged to have turned back to the microphone and announced: 'What a tremendous goal by Rumania's big blond striker Blodifino.'

Sometimes the unexpected can happen even when you're on the top of your form, the words are flowing and the play is exciting.

It happened to me quite painfully in a commentary match at Douglas Park, Hamilton a few years back involving Accies and Clydebank. Halfway through the second half one of the Hamilton players kicked the ball into touch, it cannoned off one of the floodlight pylons and hit me full in the face – and in mid sentence – as I sat in my commentary position at the front of the stand.

I felt the salt taste of blood in my mouth as teeth met soft flesh and managed to gasp, 'Oh dear, this is the first time I've ever been hit right in the face with the ball and I don't like it.' Fortunately, my teeth remained intact, so I did manage to finish the commentary without the handicap of a lisp. Nevertheless I had to have medical attention back at the studio later and made a mental note that the player responsible would not have a good game next time I was called on to see him play.

Less painful, and certainly more humorous, was an earlier occasion during commentary on a European Cup match between Ujpest Dosza and Celtic in Hungary when dignity was thrown to the wind in one calamitous moment. Before the match I noticed that the Hungarian commentators would all be standing around the track speaking into fixed microphones. Well, I didn't mind the fixed microphones, but two hours is a long time to be standing – and working – at a match, particularly since, unlike the Hungarian commentators, we

Chatting with a modern-day legend, Liverpool player-manager Kenny Dalglish before the testimonial for Celtic winger Davie Provan in 1987. Picture courtesy of John Cullen and Andy Feeney.

were not used to it. So I scouted around and managed to find two canvas chairs, one for myself and one for John Blair, of the *Sunday People,* who would be assisting with the commentary.

I did notice that both chairs were a bit shoogly, but they were all that were available and I gave it no more thought as John and I sat down to enjoy the match and the commentary. Things did not go well with Celtic. They were 3-0 down and were well into the second half when it happened. I turned to make a point about the match to John and next thing I knew the light canvas chair was moving with me.

A split second later my rather large frame – 15 stone something at the time – was lying flat on its back looking up at the dark Hungarian sky. Worse, as I turned and fell, I glanced off John's similarly flimsy chair and his 14 stones followed me to the ground where we lay side by side as the action continued furiously on the field.

We must have been a comical sight, and indeed behind us the Hungarian fans were laughing uproariously at the undignified predicament of the man from the BBC. In the split seconds that I lay supine my brain recorded that my problem was to get back to the microphone which, unlike its human component, was still proudly vertical. As I stumbled to my feet – beating John by a short head – I saw out of the corner of my eye that Jock Stein, the Celtic manager, who also occupied a trackside seat, had spotted our discomfiture and was having a good laugh to himself, too.

I suppose it said a lot for the man that he could find it in himself to laugh at all, bearing in mind how things were going for his team on the field. At any rate, rather breathlessly, I managed to blurt out to the listeners that the short break in commentary had occurred not because of some complicated technical problem with the lines from Britain but was down to two very untrustworthy chairs.

I also informed them that neither my health nor John's had been affected by our slight mishap. I understand the incident brought more than one chuckle from the listeners in Scotland and I'm glad about that. I'm also aware that few commentators would admit on the air to having fallen off their chair at the height of a European tie. It's not quite the dignified image associated with the profession.

But I could see no good reason, nor can I yet, why the public shouldn't be let into the little hazards of the job. If it made this disembodied voice addressing them from Eastern Europe seem a little more human, so much the better. An underground newspaper in Glasgow got it right a few days later. It published a cartoon of yours truly doing the Budapest backflip and, in an accompanying story, commented: 'In fairness, David Francey seemed to enjoy the incident as much as the listeners.' True.

At any rate the story has passed into Francey legend and, like others which have, perhaps, been somewhat embellished, has done me no harm.

I mention these examples only to underline that being 'on the radio' does not invest a man with infallibility. Far from it. It's a tough job. A novelist can polish and re-write his prose. A sportswriter has the safety catch of being able to read his copy before transmission, or having it checked for factual errors by a sub editor. The sports broadcaster is on his own with only the fresh air between his pronouncements and the listener. He is, in a sense, living on his wits. That said, I wouldn't have missed the last thirty years for anything.

8
Jock Stein

The streets of Cardiff were ablaze with tartan. The fans were *en fête*. We were on our way to Mexico — Scotland's fourth qualification in a row for the finals of the World Cup assured, thanks to a penalty goal by Davie Cooper, of Rangers, which earned the Scots a 1-1 draw with Wales at Ninian Park.

And now the Scottish supporters were celebrating as only they can, boisterously, good naturedly, marching through the streets of the Welsh capital to meet their buses and trains or thronging the pubs to quench that world-famous and seemingly insatiable thirst.

From the window of my taxi I spotted a group of them just up ahead, eight or nine lads, laughing, joking and singing. I asked the taxi driver to pull into the kerb, rolled down the window and, as they turned towards me, said: 'Jock's dead.' The singing stopped instantly. They just stood there and stared, bewilderment on their faces. Then they turned and walked silently away, all the jollity of the previous moments vanished.

Jock's dead. It was still difficult to comprehend. That the most enduring influence in Scottish football was truly gone and at the precise moment of yet another triumph, a cruel coincidence of circumstance that made the news even more numbing. Scotland were going to Mexico but the man who had engineered their passage, indeed would be the first Scottish international manager to achieve the finals in two successive campaigns, would not be going with them.

Jock's dead. The news flashed its way around Cardiff and the nation. Bad news travels fast and this was truly bad.

The fans, so often criticised, behaved with dignity and the respect due to one of their own whom they had lost. He was one of their own, a big, burly Lanarkshire man from Burnbank, who had known the dust of the coalfields in his native land and in South Wales and who had been plucked from this same Wales half a lifetime before and been set on a path that would make him famous and very possibly immortal.

He had come back to Wales to preside at a football match and he died doing his job. This was sad but then he will not want for an epitaph.

He went out at the top and this was appropriate for, in at least part of his playing career and certainly all of his managerial career, that was where he belonged.

A football innovator, the list of 'firsts' to his credit is a lengthy one. He gave Dunfermline Athletic their first taste of national and international success when he was the manager at East End Park. He was the only manager to lead a club to nine successive League championships, a record that, in all probability, will never now be approached, equalled or surpassed.

He was the first Scottish manager to bring the European Cup to Scotland and, to date, he remains the first and only.

And, on the night he died, he was the first to take a Scotland team among the world's elite for the second time. He ploughed a deep furrow in the national consciousness and time will not erode it.

The late Jock Stein was an intimidating presence. Ask any of the players who played for him and failed to carry out his wishes and I'm sure they would agree. Many a sports writer, too, has felt the sting of Jock's wrath for writing a particular piece, or asking a question, that was not to the big man's liking.

I incurred Stein's displeasure more than once myself. My first brush with his majestic authority came when I was still fairly new to commentating. I had been assigned to a Rangers-Celtic match at Ibrox, which is invariably a challenge to the commentator. Scottish football being what it is, an Old Firm game is always the most difficult scenario within which to convince the fans of one's strict neutrality in describing the action.

Jock Stein

Depending upon whom you offend (and you will offend someone), you're either a Bluenose So-and-So or a Fenian of questionable ancestry. Come to think of it, there are people in the game whose notions on this topic run pretty parallel to those of the fans.

At any rate there were only a few minutes of the match left when Dave Smith, Rangers' left half and one of the more elegant players on the park, was brought down by a tackle from Jimmy Johnstone, the Celtic winger. Now Jimmy is a smashing wee bloke ninety-nine per cent of the time, a friend and, in passing, simply one of the greatest wingers Scotland ever produced.

This time, though, Jimmy was in the wrong. He just stamped on Smith's ankle. In radio commentary, as I explained in an earlier chapter, you are virtually playing the game. At least that's always been my style.

The instant the incident happened, I exclaimed: 'Oh, this is ridiculous. Smith has gone down. Johnstone has deliberately stamped on his ankle. The referee will have to do something about this.'

Well, the referee did do something about it. He blew for full time two minutes early. The game was over and, as far as I was concerned, the assignment was completed and soon forgotten.

That was on a Saturday. On the following Wednesday night I travelled to Cappielow to do a report for television on a match between Morton and Celtic. As I was going in the main door at Cappielow, I came face to face with Jock Stein. 'Hello Jock,' I said. Without thinking, it seems, he said hello in return. Then I saw recognition slowly dawn in his eyes and his face suffuse with anger. 'Don't you hello Jock me,' he growled. 'You and your remarks about the referee having to take action against Jimmy Johnstsone. What about some of those fouls by Greig in the first half? Don't you ever come to me for an interview.' And he was off before I could even catch my breath or defend my comments. That incident gave me an insight into football management that I hadn't had before.

It taught me a couple of things about Stein. Since Jock couldn't have heard the broadcast (and this was in the days

The great Jock Stein and the Lisbon Lions look on as Celtic manager Billy McNeill, captain of the Lions, and David recall those memorable days. Picture courtesy of John Cullen and Andy Feeney.

before tape recordings were commonplace), he obviously had a good 'intelligence service' at work. This, I'm sure, is a prerequisite for the successful football manager, the ability to know everything that is going on in the game. Jock always had his ear close to the ground. If he was better than most of his contemporaries, it was partly because he was better informed.

There wasn't much that went on in Scottish football that Jock didn't know or hear about pretty soon after the event. And he was well aware of trends in England and abroad, as well. Not an item was written about Celtic or voiced on the air that was not spotted.

Therefore, when you were commenting on matters affecting the Parkhead club you had to be accurate and fair or face the consequences when next you met the big man. Mind you, I stand by my comments on the Smith incident. On that occasion it was Jock who was being partial, as he had every right to be. There may have been earlier provocation for Johnstone, but two wrongs don't make a right. So we had to agree to differ.

I came off second best with Jock on one other occasion. Celtic had been beaten by Airdrie at Broomfield and, at the end of the commentary, my producer asked me if I would get an interview with Stein. I argued that in the circumstances it was hardly a diplomatic request and was likely to be met with a refusal. The producer insisted. Reluctantly I made my way downstairs and knocked politely on the door of the vistiors' dressingroom. 'Yes,' said this huge figure, looking decidedly displeased with life as he was apt to be when having suffered what was in those days the unfamiliar experience of defeat.

I had probably interrupted Jock in mid-post mortem and for a minute I thought I was going to share in the home truths he had doubtless been dealing out to his players. Instead, the rebuke was short, to the point and not without some justification. 'We've won every game this season until today and you didn't ask for an interview after any of them', he said. 'Now we lose for the first time and you want an interview. No way.' I didn't argue.

Much has been said and written about Stein's tactical expertise, his ability to discern in advance the way the opposition would play and to take counter measures, his knack of getting the best out of both brilliant and ordinary players. It is true that his knowledge of the game has probably never been surpassed, at least in Britain, and indeed may never be.

But I suggest the secret of his unparalleled success as a club manager – and he was probably one of the greatest in the world – went beyond that. Jock was shrewd, intelligent, rounded. He would have been successful in any field. In addition to his knowledge of football, he had the physical presence to persuade the strongest-minded players to do his bidding, usually for their own, as well as the team's, good.

Nor did he always use confrontation tactics. Once he felt he wasn't getting a particular point through to his captain Billy McNeill, a man with very definite ideas of his own, Jock let it slip within Billy's hearing that he was thinking of giving young John Cushley an extended run at centre half 'because he'll do what I tell him.' The psychology wasn't lost on McNeill, who took the point and became Stein's strong right arm on the park in what developed into one of football's most successful partnerships.

Still, the aura of physical power was a fair weapon to have in reserve, for as Jimmy Johnstone, a player with whom Stein had his share of tribulations as well as triumphs, observed: 'You feel he could do you, really do you. You know he won't, of course, but it makes you think.'

Jock had one other gift which was developed to a degree that I had not seen in any other manager in the early days. He knew how the media worked, what it wanted or needed and, more importantly perhaps, what he wanted and needed from it. He could mould the media to his benefit. If it took kindness or bullying or whatever, Jock ensured that he captured the headlines or, more accurately, that Celtic Football Club did. He was a great publicist and entrepreneur, not so much for himself, but for the club, and many a sports writer and broadcaster had cause to be grateful that he was.

I like to think we were friends long before he died. I know for a fact that after our early disagreement he appreciated that my job obliged me to look at football in broad terms and not just from the point of view of one club.

He was a nationalist and he would help a fellow Scot, especially in the hot-house, competitive atmosphere of World Cup football. I well remember in the 1974 World Cup finals in West Germany his gesture in giving me first crack at an interview before the vital match against Yugoslavia which we needed to win to reach the quarter finals and which, in the end, we could only draw. Jock was being inundated with requests for interviews from BBC and commercial radio and TV personnel from all over the United Kingdom. He agreed to do mine first — so that the folk in Scotland who were listening would be catered for. I asked him for his prediction on the outcome and he replied: 'Davie, this is not a night for predictions. This is a night for hope!'

Again, in Liverpool when we beat Wales to qualify for the 1978 finals, Jock gave me a super interview as we walked across the Anfield pitch before the kick-off. Considering how we got off on the wrong foot in the early days, the balance was restored well in my favour before he died.

In trying to come to an overall assessment of Jock Stein's remarkable career there must be two conclusions. He was probably the best club manager ever. As an international manager I believe he was successful in a pragmatic rather than in a brilliantly dramatic manner. There are several reasons for this. For a start it is impossible to equate international success with club success.

Scotland is a small nation, and qualifying for the World Cup finals, as we have done consistently over the last dozen years, is an achievement in itself. Jock pulled off the trick for us twice, therefore the balance sheet is well in his favour even if, as was perhaps expected of him by too many people, Scotland did not win or even excel every time they took the field.

I believe he was perhaps luckier than some of his predecessors in the Scotland job in that, in deference to his innate ability and his awesome status in the game, the press and the media generally were more tolerant with him than with earlier managers. They gave him more time to settle in to the job.

That said, he continued to be an innovator when he took on his international responsibilities. Having studied the most successful international countries, he attempted the radical switch of subjugating some of our natural Scottish enthusiasm for getting the ball up the park quickly to the need for more patient and thoughtful build ups. Whether he was right to do so depends on one's view of how the game should be played or how Scotland should play it.

Bearing in mind our club system and the heavy preponderance it plays in our football, there are advantages for

Scotland's captain Roy Aitken and midfield star Paul McStay with David before a match at Parkhead. Picture courtesy of John Cullen and Andy Feeney.

the club manager that the international boss does not enjoy. These created difficulties for even the great Jock Stein. A club manager has a limited number of players under his control but they are his players and the good manager knows what makes them tick, their psychological as well as physical make-up and how to get the very best out of them.

When an international manager gets his players together they are not really his players in the true sense of the word. He does not pay their salaries which in turn pay their mortgages and therefore he does not have the total control over them that the club manager enjoys.

Additionally our overcrowded club calendar only allows our international players to get together every few months and only for a few short days. In that time the manager has to weld them into a team, a task that normally takes even the most skilled club managers years to achieve. Paradoxically, the fact that the club manager has fewer options can actually assist him in reaching the right conclusions about team blend more quickly.

Jock Stein

The international manager, with a wider range of players to choose from, can spend much more time deciding which component parts of his team link best. In fact it may take several frustrating performances before a pattern begins to emerge. I believe this happened to Jock as indeed it did to others before him.

But the man was too big and too much of a realist to let the task overawe him. He knew our national limitations better than anyone and had both the stature and the courage to enunciate them clearly before Scotland went to Spain for the 1982 finals.

It was, said Jock, an achievement that we were there and we should not harbour any delusions about winning the World Cup. He was right, of course. We do well for our size in European club competitions but handicap our national team by the excessive demands of club football. The Scotland international manager spends many an anxious Saturday night beside his telephone wondering if the players he has selected for his squad will be fit or even if they will be mentally attuned for the altogether different nature of international football. And when you are a country the size of Scotland with a sizeable proportion of your players playing in other leagues, the problem is exacerbated.

Even if we made a radical switch, decreasing the demands on our players by shortening our club season and playing fewer games, our ability to take on the best in the world would still be questionable. Jock Stein understood that and did the best he could for us, which was not at all bad.

He might have been more dramatically successful on the international scene had he taken the Scotland job at a younger age when he was at the height of his powers. We'll never know. But this brings me to my final point in remembering and paying tribute to the big man.

I think a change came over Jock after his near-fatal car crash in 1976. Until then there was an aura of invincibility about him. Nothing or no one, it seemed, could harm Jock Stein. After the crash, that changed. I don't pretend to know what went on in his mind, but I do know that a softer and more tolerant side of Jock seemed to emerge. No doubt he suffered badly, but the results of the accident were perhaps not all bad.

I think perhaps Jock got his priorities sorted out in a different way after being so close to death in that accident. Whereas before, he ate, drank and slept football, I believe he came to realise after the crash that there were other things in life besides football. He was readier to smile rather than go straight onto the offensive, altogether a more mellow man. Perhaps he lost a wee bit of his passionate commitment to the game and, by definition, something as a manager. But I believe he gained something as a person.

The night he died, Scottish football lost a massive presence. I doubt if it will ever be adequately replaced.

9
A Nice Man

The late Willie Ormond was a smashing fellow, a man who not only knew a thing or two about football management but was generous, open, warmhearted and first-class company. He did a fine job as Scotland's manager – the records show that he was probably our most successful – and he didn't get too much thanks for it.

Willie came up the hard way, a wiry wee fellow from Musselburgh, with a distinguished war record in the navy, including personal participation in the harrowing Arctic convoys which were ferrying badly needed war material to Russia.

He saw service in sunnier climes, too, and liked to recall the tale of an unfortunate shipmate with whom he shared a 'few wets' in a North African port. This chap, a fellow Scot named McKenzie, and Willie visited a few of the bars in town. A 'wet' was Willie's favourite expression for a drink, and the pair had a reasonably convivial evening before heading back for ship. Willie, sensibly, called it a night but by this time McKenzie had another appetite to assuage and, as sailors sometimes do, decided to visit a house of ill repute with the unfortunate consequence that he caught what is euphemistically termed a social disease.

The two matelots went their separate ways after that and Willie thought no more about it. Several years after the war, Ormond, by now an international winger with Hibs, was taking part in club training when a team-mate booted the ball clean out of Easter Road and onto some adjoining waste ground. Willie went to fetch the ball and there, coming towards him with the errant piece of leather in his arms was the long-lost shipmate whom he had not seen since the night he had fallen from grace in Africa.

'Ormond,' exlaimed McKenzie, recognition dawning. 'McKenzie,' replied Willie. 'How's your social disease?'

The joke was on Willie himself on an earlier occasion but, in fact, he turned what was undoubtedly a fairly humiliating experience to good use in furtherance of his footballing career. The year was 1946 and Willie, not long demobbed, had been signed for Hibs by the late Willie McCartney, a manager who was then building the Edinburgh side into one of the most talented and entertaining in Scotland. Eventually Ormond would be the left wing of an all-international forward line of Smith, Johnstone, Reilly, Turnbull and Ormond which became the toast of Scotland, the scourge of opposing defences and which helped Hibs to become champions of Scotland three times in five seasons. They were known simply as the Famous Five.

But fame, though not to be long delayed, had not yet arrived when Willie made his home debut against St Mirren. The Paisley team had at that time a somewhat slow but pugnacious full back named Miller who did not take kindly to young wingers demonstrating their artistry at his expense. Willie, excited that his big chance had come, and determined to make a good impression on his new employers, was blissfully unaware of the uncharitable streak in the nature of his immediate opponent.

Early in the game, Ormond received a pass out near the touchline and, showing a neat bit of footwork, sidestepped nimbly inside Miller's lunging tackle. Pleased with his skill, the youngster decided, on the spur of the moment, to repeat the medicine by beating the unfortunate back on the outside as well.

He never knew what hit him next as he ended up on nodding acquaintance with the track and the boundary wall, bewildered, winded and bruised in several places. As he slowly gathered his dazed wits, he was dimly aware of a familiar voice penetrating the fog of his consciousness. 'Serves you right for being a smart arse,' said the voice. 'You tried to make a monkey out of the man and you got what you deserved.' Looking into the enclosure whence the voice issued, Willie realised that the

A Nice Man

caustic comment had come from his own father, present at the game to see his son's debut and undignified comeuppance.

It was a sore lesson that it doesn't pay to mess around with an old pro, and Ormond took it to heart. From then on the fancy stuff was out. Willie concentrated on finding the shortest route to goal and became very good at it. He was a pacy, direct winger who often liked to cut inside full backs and take a pot at goal. The results were beneficial to Hibs, and Ormond blended beautifully with the other major talents around him to become an integral part of a wonderful whole.

As a player he earned plenty of bruises to add to his early painful introduction to the professional game, and he also earned international recognition, taking part in Scotland's first unhappy World Cup venture in Switzerland in 1954. Twenty years later he was given the task of leading his country to the 1974 finals in West Germany.

When Joe Jordan jumped to head that magnificent goal against Czechoslovakia on that memorable winter's evening at Hampden in 1973 which ensured Scotland's qualification for the finals for the first time in sixteen years, I can tell you the Francey frenzy was in full cry.

It was one of my happiest broadcasts. Being strictly impartial in matches between Scottish club sides may be the golden rule for commentators but, in my book, it's a fairly elastic one when it comes to describing matches involving Scotland. Objectivity must always be the aim, of course, but I would be less than honest if I said I was particularly distressed when things were going well on the park for Scotland.

At any rate, 1974 was a watershed in some respects. We'd had two pretty miserable tilts at the World Cup in the 1950s – having had the almighty cheek to decline an invitation to join the 1950 finals in Brazil because we'd finished only runners-up to England in the Home International Championship.

We'd fretted and fumed with frustration as we narrowly failed to qualify in 1962, missed out again in 1966 – when England of all countries became world champions – and sat at home again in 1970.

But now, at last, we were on our way to what we considered

our rightful place among the giants of the game, having cracked our group, which, in addition to the Czechs, who had been something of a nemesis to Scottish hopes in the past, also included Denmark.

The man chosen to lead us was the unassuming Ormond, who had cut his managerial teeth with some aplomb in the somewhat unpromising soil of Muirton Park, Perth, and Brockville. He had been appointed some eighteen months earlier to succeed the ebullient Tommy Docherty, who had left to join Manchester United.

Willie did a fine job for Scotland. The record under his stewardship is as follows:

    Played   38
    Won   18
    Drew   8
    Lost   12

That made him, statistically at least, Scotland's best international team manager to date. Yet his reign was never free of cloud or controversy.

I liked Willie enormously. More importantly, I respected his ability and judgement on football. I've known all of the Scotland managers of the last twenty years or so, and all had their special qualities.

Bobby Brown had the touch of the diplomat, a fine bearing, and he always looked as if he'd just stepped out of a bandbox, so well did he dress. He was a tremendous ambassador for his country. Ally MacLeod, before the tragedy of Argentina, was the greatest PR man we ever had. Jock Stein had charisma and authority. Tommy Docherty was aggressive and abrasive. He called his international squads hit men and for a time they brought some success. But he seemed like a man in a great hurry, like someone marking time between jobs. I remember one SFA official remarking to me just after Tommy's appointment: 'Well, we've got the Doc but I don't know for how long.' It was a prophetic remark, for Tommy's reign was short, though to be fair, he only left Park Gardens for one of the greatest jobs in football.

I worked with the Doc once or twice when he assisted with

commentaries. I would never criticise his broadcasting ability, but there were times when I felt he thought only in terms of black and white, omitting the shades of grey that are always there.

Once when we were working together during a Scotland match, Colin Jackson, the Rangers centre half, who was playing for Scotland that night, gathered the ball and instead of clearing it elected to pass to his left back, Willie Donachie, of Manchester City.

Willie was caught in possession, tackled, and, as the ball ran out of play for a throw in, I said something to the effect that Donachie had been a bit slow to collect the ball from Jackson. The Doc instantly replied: 'Well, if Colin Jackson could play football he wouldn't have given the boy that pass in the first place.'

My own view is that any player who can hold down his job for his club over the years and be selected to represent his country is entitled to think he can play football, irrespective of what Tommy Docherty might say or think.

But that was the Doc, always tough, abrasive and quick with his judgements. He doesn't seem to have changed much.

Ormond was a different type entirely, quieter, more reflective but lucky in two respects. He had either been born with, or had developed, the knack of picking players who would play well together. I had many long conversations with Willie, particularly on foreign trips, an environment in which he often seemed somehow lonely. Time and time again he would say that anyone could pick the eleven best players available to an international team. The trick was to find the right blend. I think the wee man found it more often than not.

I believe he was fortunate in one other respect, in having a generation of players who were, on the whole, more talented than, say, the squad available to Andy Roxburgh today.

This is a personal view but I think it has some weight when you consider a sample of the names involved: Billy Bremner, Jimmy Johnstone, Kenny Dalglish, Danny McGrain, David Hay, Joe Jordan, Peter Lorimer and Denis Law, though admittedly the great Denis was past his best.

David and former Scotland manager, the late Willie Ormond, whom he describes as a smashing wee fellow.

Balancing out the good luck for Ormond was the other side of a coin that seemed to see him with a constant fight on his hands to win the outright confidence of his employers. Perhaps the fact that Willie was never bombastic or 'political' worked against him in the temper of the times. Certainly the disciplinary image of the Scotland squad was none too hot in the period.

Before we even embarked for West Germany, Jimmy Johnstone, the controversial Celtic winger, gave the newspapers a field day with the famous late-night rowing-boat incident at Largs which had the lifeguards doing a spot of unscheduled overtime. Bremner, the captain, and Johnstone were later involved in an after-curfew drinking row in Oslo *en route* to the finals and when, the following year, Bremner, Joe Harper, Willie Young, Arthur Graham and Pat McCluskey were banned *sine die* from playing for Scotland after another nocturnal episode in Copenhagen, it began to look as though a sizeable proportion of Scottish international footballers were nothing more than Hooray Henrys, using their status as a free ride to making whoopee. Yet, to me, they were all marvellous chaps.

Mind you, in retrospect it is easier to see that these well-publicised incidents reflected more discredit on the players concerned than on a fair-minded manager inclined to treat them as responsible adults rather than ride censorious shotgun on troublesome children.

Every international manager must feel at some time that his job is on the line and Ormond, perhaps, more than most. I well remember that famous trip to Rumania in 1975 for a European Championship qualifying match, a journey which must have been a sore trial to the wee man. Jock Stein had been appointed to the charge of the Scotland Under-21 team, and having a towering figure like the then Celtic manager at one's shoulder is hardly likely to make any manager feel totally secure in his job.

Whether Willie felt, as many of us did, that Jock would step in if asked, I don't know. But I'm sure the SFA's decision to call up the most famous and successful manager in the land didn't do much to reassure the incumbent about his long-term future.

I got a hint of the way Willie's mind was working just after the Under-21s had played the Rumanian Under-21s on the Tuesday before Wednesday's big game. We could have had a real going over in that match. The referee was an Eastern European and he gave the young Rumanians everything. They were all over the Scots and then, in just about our only attack, Alfie Conn, one of the few players to play for both Rangers and Celtic, but then with Tottenham, scored.

After that the Rumanians threw everything at us. Somehow our goal survived intact, and minutes from the end a Rumanian shot which looked net-bound seemed to be turned round the post by a Scottish defender's hand. For once, the referee gave Scotland a break. He gave a corner. We won 1-0, much against the run of play.

Back at the Scotland hotel later that night I went up to

Willie's room for a chat and found the wee man lying on top of his bed in his underpants. Before I could say a word he said: 'You saw that game this afternoon, David. One thing you've got to say about Jock. He's a lucky big bastard.'

This was the same trip during which Rankin Grimshaw, of Raith Rovers, who was then president of the SFA, announced to the Press that the Association were not satisfied that the manager was getting as much out of the players as he might. In my view it was a shocking error of judgement on the part of a leading official, as such a public statement, made in a foreign country, could only undermine the manager's position.

Ormond had to suffer the acute embarrassment of sitting beside Jock Stein on the plane on the way home knowing that the knives were out for him in high places. We did not qualify for those European Championship finals. As a matter of fact we never have in this particular competition. But Ormond survived the whispers — or was it a shout? — and to his credit carried on doing his job to the best of his ability. But he quit the Scotland post without too much regret when a club position offered itself with Hearts. Incidentally, the score in Rumania was 1-1, not a bad result by any means in inhospitable Eastern Europe, and certainly one Scotland would not sniff at today.

Before Ormond returned to club management, however, he had the satisfaction of leading his country to the World Cup finals in West Germany. From a Scottish point of view these were probably the happiest finals that we have been involved in in the modern era.

Although I had commentated on many World Cup qualifying matches, 1974 marked my own debut in the finals and I looked forward immensely to being a part of the strong British radio team from the BBC who would cover the finals. I wasn't disappointed. When we got to Germany the controversial build up to the finals was forgotten. The team, officials, press, radio and television were as one in wanting the best for Scotland, everyone desperately anxious for us to give a good account of ourselves as a country after an absence of sixteen years from the world's premier stage.

A Nice Man

It was a great trip. Before our final and crucial match against Yugoslavia I could hardly credit the number of well kent faces I saw outside the Wald Stadium in Frankfurt. It seemed just about every manager in Scotland, many of our leading coaches and not a few players had come to cheer the boys on. Our patriotic hopes were high that we would qualify for the ultimate stages in that pleasant summer of 1974.

Well, we'll never get closer to reaching the last eight. In the end a goal difference of one, a piece of bumpy German turf, a tactical gaffe and a gentleman named Kasadi kept us out of the ultra elite.

Remember Kasadi? He was the goalkeeper of Zaire, the no hopers of Group 2. The Africans had been lumped in with the Scots, the powerful Yugoslavs and Brazil, who although they were in something of a transitional situation by their own towering standards, were always to be feared. Compared to these experienced footballing countries, Zaire were like innocents abroad.

Ormond had already come to that conclusion. The manager had done his homework on the World Cup newcomers by watching them in a qualifying match against Egypt in Cairo. It did not take him long to conclude that they were enthusiastic but naive and not equipped to survive in the rarefied atmosphere of the World Cup. They would not present a problem to Scotland.

He was right except for two things. The ebony-skinned Kasadi had one of those nights when everything went right and Billy Bremner, Scotland's influential captain, evidently did not share the manager's opinion that Zaire could be taken totally to the cleaners.

On the face of it, Scotland seemed lucky to draw the Africans in their opening match in the Westphalia Stadium in Dortmund while the two other strong teams in the group kicked off against each other. With hindsight we might have been better to play them later on. At any rate, things began well for the Scots when Peter Lorimer, of Leeds, put them ahead early in the match with a thunderbolt shot of the kind he loved to produce. His team-mate big Joe Jordan scored another soon after and we were well on our way.

But although he had been beaten twice early on Kasadi emerged as a man more than equal to the task. Like an inspired acrobat he jumped around his goal, frustrating the Scots in their efforts to add to their score with a series of fine saves. The man seemed unbeatable.

Perhaps this frustration had a bearing on Bremner's decision to ask his men at half-time to keep it tight and hold what they had already achieved rather than risk losing a goal at the other end. At any rate we won comfortably enough though without the barrowload of goals we looked capable of scoring early in the game.

With hindsight it is easy to be critical of Bremner's decision, which was undoubtedly made from the best motives. But had the Scots exerted the pressure of which they were capable, it is highly possible that Kasadi's resolve would have melted, bearing in mind what was to happen to the goalkeeper within the space of a few days. We'll never know, though I believe the holding policy decided upon at half-time was a crucial factor in the story as it unfolded.

As Yugoslavia and Brazil had played a scoreless draw in their opening match, Scotland were temporarily group leaders and the next assignment was to face the might of Brazil at the Wald Stadium. This was perhaps one of the finest and most disciplined performances by a Scottish team on a foreign field as we matched the inventiveness of the Brazilians from the word go and bettered them in effort.

Bremner was an inspirational captain, urging his men on from midfield, and it was particularly tragic that he should be the central figure in the best chance to win the match and the game's biggest missed opportunity. With only minutes remaining and the teams deadlocked without a score, the ball was played across the face of the Brazilian goal, reaching Bremner almost on the line.

'It must be a goal,' I roared in commentary, or something to that effect. But the ball took a split second bounce off the turf just as Billy stabbed at it and it came off his foot and went wide. It was a chance, no doubt, but a fleeting one and

A Nice Man

certainly never as easy as it would have appeared to us in the commentary box or the television viewers back home. I have sympathy with players who find themselves in that situation and I had sympathy with Bremner that night.

For while it is a privilege to commentate on football, the ultimate responsibility for results rests with the players and it is a heavy one. Sitting perhaps a hundred yards removed from the scene, it is impossible to be aware of all the factors that can contribute to a seemingly easy chance missed.

At any rate Scotland had done themselves and their reputation as fighters no harm in that stirring contest with Brazil. The awful thing was that Mr Kasadi had proved himself not only human but of doubtful competence by losing nine goals to the Yugoslavs, who, in terms of goal difference, were now in a class of their own.

I watched the Yugoslavia-Zaire match in the Press centre later on and could not believe that this was the same goalkeeper who had defied Scotland. He gifted the Slavs three goals in the time it takes for players to loosen up their muscles and I could not only have saved all three but also caught the ball by the lace for the third. And, remember, in 1974 I was 50!

The upshot of that Yugoslav landslide, added to our failure to punish the African side sufficiently, was that we had to beat Yugoslavia in the final match or, in the event of getting a scoring draw, hope, somehow, that Zaire would not surrender any more than two goals to Brazil.

Both hopes were fairly slim, as we now had the measure of Zaire's mettle and knew that Yugoslavia were a tough proposition. So it proved. Up in the commentary box I had my thoughts on two games as my studio feed kept giving me the unwanted information: 'Brazil are leading Zaire 1-0,' 'Brazil have gone two up,' 'Brazil have scored a third.' Not even the substitution of the hapless Kasadi by a fresh 'keeper for this game could help our cause. The Scotland-Yugoslavia match was a tense struggle between two evenly matched teams, the only difference being that a draw would enable the Eastern Europeans to qualify for the last eight. They got that, scoring near the end with Joe Jordan salving Scottish pride with a last-

Sharing a chat during a trip to West Germany with Gerry McNee, of the *Scottish Daily Express* and Radio Clyde.

minute equaliser.

We were out. But unbeaten and unbowed. Sad but not dispirited. West Germany had been a bittersweet experience for Scotland, the only team to fail to qualify for the last stages without losing a match. We had returned to the world stage from long exile and had given a good account of ourselves.

I had enjoyed my commentaries and entered into the general spirit of things in the Scottish camp. There were no hangdog looks on the SFA charter plane back to Scotland. I can even remember Willie Allan, then SFA secretary and an austere man, joining heartily in the chorus of 'Six foot two, eyes of blue, Big Jim Holton's after you.' Someone must have spiked his coffee.

It was the high point of Willie Ormond's managerial career. Like Jock Stein he is gone now. Like Stein, too, prematurely, and we are the poorer for it.

But on the way home from Germany we knew we'd be back challenging the world in four years' time. We didn't know that a modern-day Pied Piper would take us there and that he would charm an entire nation into grandiose ideas of conquest with the eloquence of his song.

10

Midsummer Madness in Argentina

Ally McLeod was perhaps the greatest PR man the Scotland international team has ever had. That said, he let himself and his country down. He made a rash prediction about our chances in the 1978 World Cup finals in Argentina and could not live up to it. He did not do his homework sufficiently well before entering the toughest arena in world football. He built a nation up to a level of expectancy verging on hysteria and then watched helplessly as the hopes he had raised were cruelly dashed.

Mind you, we were all — or most of us — accomplices of Ally in the greatest piece of self-deception it has been my misfortune to experience in thirty-five years of involvement with football.

Argentina was to be our vindication as a leading member of the community of footballing nations. It became Scotland's sporting Vietnam.

But if we were left with a monumental sense of let down, the build up certainly was a lot of fun for a lot of people. Ally MacLeod had inherited the Scotland job from Willie Ormond after a full and varied career as a player, and he had a managerial pedigree which proved he could enliven club environments as diverse as Ayr United and Aberdeen, blend winning teams and motivate players.

Outgoing and confident in both his own and his players' ability, he was a good choice for the job and a popular one both with the football establishment and the man in the street. He had a good squad of players at his disposal, too, and the qualifying draw was kind to Scotland.

Czechoslovakia, our qualifying victims in 1974, seemed the main danger again in a group that was three-quarters British with Northern Ireland and Wales completing the quartet.

We survived a defeat in Prague to win the group once more at the expense of the Czechs, the Irish and the Welsh but only after considerable controversy in the qualifying match against Wales at Anfield. Did Joe Jordan handle the ball in the controversial incident in which we were awarded a decisive penalty? Joe swears to this day that he didn't but you'll never find a Welshman who doesn't think otherwise.

But Wales had to remain at home and dream of might-have-beens. Scotland were Britain's only representatives in the southern hemisphere in 1978 since England, too, had failed to qualify for the second time running. Perhaps this helped to fuel the national ego. England's absence was noted in a record cut by Scots comedian Andy Cameron who sang 'We're on the march with Ally's Army' with chauvinistic gusto.

Sheila and I, visiting our son and daughter-in-law at the time, found our oldest grandson marching up and down the livingroom floor singing the words of the song. He was then three years of age. Sheila asked him if his dad had taught him the words and he replied: 'No, my other gran did'.

Ally MacLeod, beating the publicity drum for all it was worth, had the entire country behind him and his team, from three-year-old toddlers to grandmothers caught up in a wave of football fever.

There was a kind of midsummer madness in the air. Ally said he believed we would get a medal in Argentina and a lot of people believed him. I remember that I even vaguely cherished a dream that we might win the World Cup.

Of course when you consider all the great teams who would be in Argentina along with us, there was not the slightest chance that Scotland would win it. But people were not thinking in those terms that summer.

Scotland even had a heroes' send off before a ball was kicked, with the team, officials and manager cheered onto the pitch at Hampden, which was opened to the public, before they boarded the bus for Prestwick airport and the SFA charter flight to Argentina. It was a great show, a morale booster and a wonderful public relations act.

Midsummer Madness in Argentina

All the way to the airport crowds lined the streets to give the team an emotional farewell. It really was a moving experience, even for those of us who would not be playing. I remember Willie Harkness, the then president of the SFA, remarking: 'This is my VE day all over again'. I was old enough to know what he meant but I'm sure the remark went over the heads of a lot of the players who were from a younger generation.

The real business, though, lay ahead. If a defeat by England at Hampden in the Home International Championships, which was the prelude to leaving for Argentina, was a pointer that Scotland were far from invincible, no one seemed to pay too much attention. Peru and Iran had to be disposed of and, if we could get a result against Holland, who appeared the main threat to our chances — as indeed we did — then Scotland would be through to the final stages and that dream of a medal would be that much closer.

Ally was confident. Asked about Peru, he joked: 'Who's Peru?'

In fact, like any South American team, Peru had to be taken seriously. Video recordings of their qualifying matches, which the Scots watched at their Dunblane Hydro headquarters before leaving for South America and again at their Alta Gracia headquarters in Argentina, seemed to confirm their potential danger, though this did not diminish the Scots' confidence that they would win their opening match in Cordoba.

Peru appeared to be a useful side on the break, though vulnerable in defence and less than adept at dealing with high balls into the goalmouth. That at least was the conclusion of my TV colleagues who had studied the recordings.

The day before the match I was having a beer with a Peruvian journalist who gave me pause for thought. He said Peru had a winger named Munante, whose pace would leave the Scottish defence standing, and a midfield player, Cubillas, who would orchestrate the play. Peru would win, he said.

That is exactly what happened. Munante was a flier, Cubillas tormented the Scots, and a 3-1 defeat brought our dreams back down to earth. At home, I'm told, folk were stunned. Likewise those who were on the spot. Stewart Kennedy, of

Aberdeen, who played at right back for Scotland that day, told me that he had never faced a player as fast as Munante in his life. Inevitably, the recriminations began. Why had Scotland, and the manager in particular, failed to take Peru seriously? Just how good were Scotland anyway? And yet the cause was not yet beyond redemption. Now we had to play Iran and surely they would present no problems for the Scots. With good results against the no hopers from the Middle East and against Holland, Scotland could still qualify for the second stage.

We didn't known then that something far worse than losing to Peru was lying in wait around the corner.

I was having a day off a couple of days before the match against Iran and was relaxing at my hotel in Cordoba when I got a phone call from a BBC producer in Buenos Aires telling me there was a problem at the Scottish camp in nearby Alta Gracia. It was, he said, a drugs scandal involving Willie Johnston. Would I get up to Alta Gracia and check it out?

By coincidence I had interviewed Johnston only the day before. Willie was a good player and a good talker and he seemed a good candidate for an interview, and our chat for the record had gone well, except for one thing. He had a streaming cold and was taking aspirins to alleviate the problem.

I told the producer that I thought I knew the answer, that Willie had been taking medication for his cold and this had probably shown up in the random drug test. Anyway I got to the press conference to discover that Johnston had been taking Reactivan tablets — a banned stimulant — and that a drug test had proved positive. He was being sent home in disgrace.

It was another bombshell in the Scottish camp and the disclosure could scarcely have come at a worse time from the point of view of morale. I was sorry for Johnston, who was then playing for West Brom. I'm certain he wasn't the kind of chap who would deliberately take tablets to flout the rules. But if he was still feeling as bad as he looked when I interviewed him, he probably took the Reactivan as a means of giving himself a lift.

Another Scotland player, midfielder Don Masson, a pal of Johnston's, also confessed to Ally McLeod to taking Reactivan

Midsummer Madness in Argentina

With an LP of his commentary on the occasion of Rangers winning the treble of League, League Cup and Scottish Cup in season 1975-6. He also recorded an LP of famous Celtic European and Cup wins. Picture courtesy of *Mercury and Advertiser*.

and then denied it, and although he wasn't sent home he didn't play for Scotland again.

It's impossible to gauge the effect of the drugs revelations on the mental preparedness of the team for the next crucial match against Iran. I would not have thought they would have helped the Scots. Certainly we were now having manpower problems. Johnston had gone, there was no Masson and the team captain Bruce Rioch was unfit.

The absence of Rioch, an influential player, was a big blow, and when Martin Buchan, another key player, went off injured before half-time the little rhythm the Scots had managed to find vanished altogether.

The game against Iran, which ended in a 1-1 draw and virtually ended our hopes of making any impression in Argentina, was a miserable experience. It was the worst

Scotland performance I have ever seen and I have commentated on many indeed. There were only 8,000 folk in the stadium, the poorest crowd of the entire finals.

Although we drew 1-1 we didn't even score. An own goal put Scotland ahead, so it was the Iranians who scored twice. In one of their few attacks an Iranian beat Archie Gemmill out on the left before hitting a low angled shot which beat Alan Rough at his near post, always a bad type of goal for a 'keeper to lose.

I believe the first time around I gave the goal to Andravik whereas Eskendarian scored it. From 150 yards distance it is difficult to tell one player from another in an unfamiliar team and I don't suppose it mattered much anyway to the listeners in Kilwinning or Kilbarchan.

Perversely, there was still just the glimmer of hope that a goal glut against Holland would edge the Scots through to the quarter final stage, though that seemed an unlikely occurrence indeed. In fact, our hopes were raised when we scored three and went into a 3-1 lead in our final game in Mendoza.

Scotland needed to win by three clear goals to join Peru in the second stage at the expense of Holland, and their hopes soared with their finest performance in Argentina, embellished by a marvellous individual goal from Archie Gemmill, officially recognised later as the finest score of the tournament. But Holland's Johnny Rep smashed in a long-range goal late in the game to bring the result to 3-2 and kill Scotland's chances.

Once again we were eliminated on goal difference, Holland going through with Peru, though the eventual winners would be the host nation Argentina.

I did not enjoy Argentina as much as I had West Germany. I felt the team had let the country down, though the miserable performances against Peru and Iran were redeemed to some extent by the defiant win over Holland, even though that turned out to be meaningless. I continued to enjoy commentary, of course, but I wasn't particularly well in Argentina. I had a chest cough which bothered me for weeks after I returned, I was tired while I was there and frankly towards the end a little homesick after being away from Scotland in such an alien environment for three and a half weeks. I believe everyone was ready for

Midsummer Madness in Argentina

home at the finish.

However, in my case, even the homecoming was to be less than straightforward. Having stayed overnight in Mendoza after the game with Holland, an early morning flight was needed to take me to Buenos Aires to catch the plane home with the official Scottish party. Incredibly, and as if Argentina were saying 'I'm not finished with you yet!' I awoke on the morning of the flight to find Mendoza shrouded in as thick a blanket of fog as any old-fashioned pea-souper I had experienced in Glasgow.

Panic reigned. You see, the problem was that the Scottish party did not have a charter plane as was the case in trips to Europe. Due to the enormous expense of chartering a whole plane for a trip to Argentina, a block booking of seats had been taken on a service flight. So whereas a chartered plane could be held back to accommodate latecomers, no such luxury was afforded them on a service aircraft.

As I stood fuming in Mendoza Airport swallowing coffee by the pint, the huge airport clock, the focus on my near-hypnotised stare, spelt out its message. The time had come and gone for the scheduled aircraft to sail into the clear blue skies of Buenos Aires, destined for my beloved Scotland, and here was I trapped in an unknown Argentinian town a mere half hour's flight away.

Eventually, seemingly having had its fun, the weather changed dramatically. The town and airport of Mendoza were drenched in sunlight and I clambered aboard the aircraft to Buenos Aires with one thought in mind, the shortest route from Buenos Aires to Glasgow.

The airport officials at the huge international airport of Buenos Aires were courteous, sympathetic, but powerless to get me on to a direct flight to London in less than two days hence. This in my present state of frustration was totally unacceptable. After hours of discussion with every operating company in the airport, a solution was presented by an official of the Swiss Airline. I would fly to Lucerne that evening, catch a London connection next day, and thence to Glasgow.

Such had been my single-minded application to the

problem of getting home that it was not until I was seated on the plane for Switzerland that the thought struck me, and struck me forcibly. Surely my luck had changed with a vengeance. I was scheduled to land at Lucerne and, believe it or not, Sheila, my wife, was holidaying with friends at Lake Lucerne. Naturally my first move on landing was to telephone the hotel where Sheila was staying. My luck had not, after all, changed. 'Mrs. Francey's party left the hotel for home this morning' I was told.

I had been home three days when I received a telephone call from the BBC in London. 'Thank God we've found you. We've been chasing you half way around the world — We thought you had disappeared.' The powers that be were far from pleased. In retrospect, maybe I should have contacted them. At the time I had more important things on my mind.

Truly, 'Midsummer Madness' it was.

Scotland returned from Argentina in a chastened mood which contrasted sharply with the ballyhoo which had surrounded their departure. Ally MacLeod was given a vote of confidence by his bosses at the SFA and could have stayed in the job and given it another go. But Argentina took an emotional toll of him, I doubt if his heart was really in it after the traumas he endured during those eventful weeks, and in any case it was probably time for a new man to take on the job.

A new pragmatic era in Scottish international football was about to dawn with the appointment of Jock Stein. Ally MacLeod was a one-off, an international team manager who was bold enough — or foolish enough — to make predictions about a game that defies forecasts. He opened a Pandora's Box of troubles for himself in so doing.

I don't think the fans forgave him for failing to deliver what he seemed to promise. He returned to the comparative tranquillity of club management. But for a time he united a country in the common belief that they were good enough to take on the world. We have been to two World Cup finals since but never with the excitement that was generated in 1978.

Argentina was also a watershed in my own career. I didn't know it at the time but they would be my last World Cup finals

Midsummer Madness in Argentina

What the well dressed radio commentator was wearing in 1978. David models the BBC official uniform for the World Cup finals in Argentina. Picture courtesy of the *Mercury and Advertiser.*

as a broadcaster. I was accredited by the BBC initially for the finals in Spain in 1982 and the first I knew that I would not be going was when a reporter from the *Evening Times* rang me to tell me the news.

The Glasgow *Evening Times* ran a story saying the most famous voice on radio had been silenced. Later a spokesman for Radio 2 confirmed that the BBC would not be using David Francey in Spain, adding: 'This does not mean to say we won't use him in the future. If people in Scotland are unhappy we are sorry but this is a decision of the BBC.'

David Begg went to Spain to do the commentaries instead and I never did get an explanation as to why I was left out, although I did hear on the grapevine that it was thought my voice was 'too parochial.' I must say this surprised me.

I was told why I would not be in Mexico in 1986 by Malcolm Kellard, Head of Sport in Scotland. The commentators, said Malcolm, would all be supplied by Radio 2 while Denis Law, the former Scotland star, would supply the Scottish voice. Someone else would do foot-in-the-door reporting, which was not really my scene. I had, by the way, done all Scotland's qualifiers.

Of course from a professional point of view I was disappointed. But by 1986 it didn't make much difference to me. I had travelled the world, I wasn't getting any younger and it simply meant I could enjoy the World Cup in the privacy of my home. Any broadcaster will tell you that spending a large part of one's life living in hotels is not all it's cracked up to be.

And I'd had two World Cups and some wonderful memories. No one could take that away.

11
Surviving in a Tough Business

In the freelance world of broadcasting, broadcasters come and go with a regularity that can become monotonous. And when one has survived for thirty-five years, one has clearly seen a lot come and go.

Of course there are many other great survivors in the business and one of the many commentators with whom I have enjoyed working is Brian Moore. Brian, to my mind, is one of the few commentators who made a successful transition from radio to television. He has managed to retain

David in his favourite position at one of his favourite grounds, the commentary box at Hampden just before the start of the 1987 Scottish Cup Final between St Mirren and Dundee United.

the racy excitement of the radio commentary without seeming to intrude on the viewer's enjoyment of seeing for himself what is happening. I believe that in football particularly, fans, and therefore the viewers, regard themselves as specialists and in that sense it really is the people's game. Whereas in many other sports a commentator can explain the obvious and appear the more knowledgeable for so doing, a football commentator applying the same principle attracts only loudly voiced criticism. 'Does he think we're blind or something?'

My first working engagement with Brian was when we shared the European Cup final in unforgettable Lisbon in 1967 when Celtic beat Inter Milan 2-1. I believe our styles complemented each other well and indeed I can only remember one blunder apiece which, considering we shared some two hours' live broadcasting in a cauldron-like atmosphere, wasn't too bad.

My boob was, of course, one which has been regularly aired over the years — 'The Glasgow voices could be heard in the streets of Lisbon all night long ringing out that well known anthem, 'There's not a team like the GLASGOW RANGERS.'' Brian's startled look at this utterance made me realise immediately that that was no way to talk about Celtic. The correction was hurriedly made.

I was happy to be able to reciprocate later in the game when Brian awarded Celtic's winning goal to 'Murdock.' My instinctive 'It was Stevie Chalmers' had that cultured voice announcing without a pause 'And indeed David Francey tells me the scorer was Steve Chalmers.'

I am delighted that Brian Moore, a charming and top-class professional, has achieved such outstanding success, even if it has been with 'the opposition.'

The best-known football commentator on television in the very early days was, of course, Kenneth Wolstenholme. Although we never worked together, the fact that we covered the same games, Ken for television, I for radio, meant that we spent a fair bit of time in each other's company. Ken was physically a big, good-looking man who also thought and acted big. I do not mean that in an unkind sense but, as a relatively new boy in the globetrotting scene I could not be

It's all over at Hampden and David gets a hand on the coveted Scottish Cup alongside Alex Smith, manager of the victorious St Mirren team in 1987.

other than impressed by this established figure who had been broadcasting games of the calibre of Real Madrid against Eintracht Frankfurt when I was a mere terracing spectator.

One factor struck me forcibly about Kenny Wolstenholme from our first meeting. Harking back to something I've already mentioned in a previous chapter, I have often been asked by listeners who don't know me very well how I manage to go through an entire commentary without swearing.

The answer, as I've already explained, is that I don't swear in everyday life. Wolstenholme is very different. His everyday language could be startlingly rough. Indeed, during any typical evening 'with the boys' he rarely uttered a sentence which was not highly coloured. And yet here was a man who could broadcast in highly volatile situations with never a deviation from the Queen's English. Considering his partiality to swear words when off duty, this was a remarkable achievement.

I was sad and disappointed for Ken when he told me one day that he believed his days with the BBC were coming to an end. He had come to Glasgow for a Scotland-England game. I was covering the game for radio and I arranged to pick him up at the Royal Stuart Hotel. In the taxi on the way to Hampden he told me that moves were afoot in London to replace him.

Because of his 'name,' which was very big indeed, and also the quality of his work, I found it hard to believe. But it was true. The replacement he told me about was rapidly to become a household name himself and remains so to this day. He was David Coleman.

Coleman's sheer professionalism is a quality I have always admired. A superb commentator on athletics as well as football, as far as I could see he left absolutely nothing to chance. I recall an official lunch in Germany before a Scotland game hosted by the German football authorities. David had been invited but did not turn up and his absence was noted. When one of our hosts asked about him, a TV colleague offered an apology and pointed out that David was resting before the game.

In Argentina before the opening of the 1978 World Cup finals I saw another example of that professionalism. Scotland's opening game against Peru on 1st June was scheduled for Cordoba and for that reason those who would be broadcasting the game were based there.

The official World Cup ceremony to mark the opening of the finals was to take place in the magnificent River Plate Stadium in Buenos Aires some 435 miles away. David Coleman was to be the commentator for the opening ceremony on national television.

Three days before the opening ceremony a few of us were having dinner in a rather pleasant restaurant in Cordoba but I could see that David was not at one with the world. The explanation came later in the evening as nature called us both at the same time. In the relative seclusion of the washroom

Surviving in a Tough Business

At the shrine of Scottish football again, this time with fellow commentator Jock Brown, now STV's chief football voice but then with the BBC. Picture courtesy of the Rangers News.

David told me that the powers that be in the BBC expected him to broadcast the event without his being able to attend the rehearsal the day before. 'Do you know their excuse, David?' he asked me. Then, without waiting for a reply or even for a shake of my head, he went on: 'There is not a scheduled plane which can get me to Buenos Aires in time.'

He then came out with his own rather spectacular solution. 'I've just told them if there's not a scheduled civilian plane, get a bloody military plane!'

David Coleman attended the rehearsal and made his usual immaculate job of the official ceremony.

In my commentaries it was only for special events, internationals, cup finals or European ties that I was joined in the commentary box by a summariser, or analyst as they are now called. Presumably this was for reasons of finance. Whatever the reason for restricting the analyst to special events, it was a very good idea to have one, for a good analyst is a very useful addition to a commentary team. While the commentator is following the ball and is, therefore, somewhat restricted in his view of the tactical side of the game, the analyst can take an overall view and provide listeners with this extra dimension.

Many of Scotland's well-known sports journalists have been used in this role. Ian Archer, the *Glasgow Herald's* Jim Reynolds and Ian Paul, Allan Herron of the *Sunday Mail*, the *Scottish Sunday Express's* Phil McEntee and Ken Robertson and John Blair, formerly of *The People* and now the SFA's press officer, have all rendered yeoman service.

Recently a more permanent fixture in the role has been former Scotland and Rangers captain John Greig. Greigy's forthright, honest and knowledgeable approach to the game has brought him many listening fans even in quarters where he was less than appreciated as a player.

Incidentally, there is no truth in the story that I demanded that, before I would work with John, the BBC would require to supply me with a pair of shinguards!

To conclude on the subject of football broadcasters, I should say that Jock Brown, of Scottish Television, is a commentator who, like Brian Moore, made a very successful transition from radio to television.

Jock, a lawyer and the brother of Craig Brown, Scotland's assistant manager, and I first shared commentary some years ago before he moved over to TV. He is a good, racy commentator who manages to convey the overall picture without encroaching on the viewer's ability to see for himself what is going on.

I would anticipate that Jock will be the top Scottish Television football commentator for many years to come.

Lord Barnett, P.C., Vice Chairman, BBC Board of Governors, presents a framed cover of the *Radio Times* after the Scottish Cup Final between Aberdeen and Hearts in 1986 to David, who provided radio commentary on the match. Picture courtesy of *Radio Times*.

Cheers! With Brian Moore at a recent function.

12

Teuchter for a Day

On Wednesday, 1st June, 1983, I received a telephone call from the then senior producer of Radio Sport, Murdoch McPherson. The fact of the call was commonplace because Murdoch and I kept contact even during football's close season. What was not commonplace was the producer's request: 'I'd like you to provide commentary on Saturday on the Camanachd Cup Final.'

'But that's shinty.'

'Well, there's a book of rules in the post to you. You'll cope all right. And by the way, the game is sponsored by Glenmorangie Whisky and they'd like you to reply on behalf of the guests at the official dinner after the game.'

Now the thought of the after-dinner speech didn't worry me because I've done a few of those in my time. But frankly, not only did I know nothing about shinty but I had never even seen a shinty match in my life. It seemed inappropriate that by way of introduction to it I should be required to broadcast a 90-minute blow by blow account of the final of the sport's most prestigious tournament. I approached the assignment with some trepidation.

My fears were hardly allayed by my first cursory glance through the *Handbook of the Camanachd Association*. I could only fervently hope that the Scottish Gaels who follow the game liked what they were going to hear in my broadcast. If I may quote, the Handbook stated: 'It [shinty] makes demands on stamina, on soundness of wind and limb, on brains as well as muscle, on prowess, on manliness and on courage, for which, in few other games, will a parallel be found.'

I found myself thinking: 'What if these guys were told by their friends that I had made some unacceptable statements about their play during the commentary?'

Might not that famed Highland hospitality turn to thoughts of retribution of a physical kind against this interloping Lowlander? I'm not a coward but neither do I seek unpleasantness for its own sake. The thought of hulking shinty players, fired with the wine of the region, on a rampage of revenge against a hapless radio commentator bothered me somewhat.

My worry did not decrease as I continued to read the handbook: 'Naturally it is no pastime for weaklings or degenerates, nor is it an exercise wherein the slow witted or dullards will be found to shine. It calls for physical and mental gifts of no mean order. It calls into play practically all the chief muscles of the human body ... etc, etc.'

There was nothing else for it but to do one's best. Having digested the facts that a shinty stick is called a caman, the field of play is around 170 yards by 80 yards, there are 12 players a side, kicks become hits and the kick off is called a throw up, I was ready to take Claggan Park, Fort William, by storm.

I loved every minute of it. Ably assisted by BBC shinty experts George Slater and Hugh Dan McLennan, I managed to keep the listeners happy. I had one anxious moment at the dinner that night as a massive, kilted gentleman lurched towards me, some intent evidently on his mind. I needn't have worried. 'I was listening as well as watching,' he said. 'That was a real professional performance you gave. I didn't know you were a shinty man.'

Then, taking a mighty swig of Glenmorangie from the huge silver Camanachd Cup, he swayed away before I could mouth a suitable word of thanks.

For the record, the score was Strachur 2, Kyles Athletic 3, and the match made a little bit of history as the first Camanachd Cup Final ever to feature two teams from Argyllshire.

13

Who'd Be a Referee?

Very few referees are popular with the fans. But then even Solomon had his critics. Some say that the referee's job is made more difficult by the fact that the rules of the Scottish Football Association prevent his explaining his decisions after the game. Mind you, I have still to be convinced that a referee giving a hotly disputed penalty in the closing minutes of a clash between, say, Rangers and Celtic, could readily calm the tempers of the penalised by an explanation, however logical.

Tom Wharton, a man whose 6ft 4inch frame dominated Scottish refereeing for many years, was in favour of the rule of silence. Having handled games in countries where referees could be questioned by the media, he told me that, in certain South American countries for example, it was a positively frightening experience to be pinned against a wall with microphones pushed into one's face while mobs of media men hurled questions.

And if the gigantic 'Tiny' Wharton found it frightening, how would some of our other referees of lesser stature fare? Like, for instance, the not very large official who refereed a game between Kilmarnock and Dundee United at Rugby Park. At the time Killie had a superb little left winger called Jim Cook. By little, I mean 5ft 2inches. Jim's diminutive body, however, held the heart of a lion, and an aggressive one at that.

For the third time in the game Jim's aggression boiled over on one Davie Wilson, 5ft 5inches in height, an erstwhile Rangers and Scotland winger playing out his illustrious career with the Tangerines.

Now Davie, who related the incident to me some time later, is alleged to have been nominated for many an Oscar for his fine portrayals of a grievously attacked man when tackled in

Congratulating Brian McClair, then of Celtic, on his being voted Scotland's Player of the Year for season 1986-7. Picture courtesy of Frank Tocher, Programme Publications.

opponents' penalty areas.

On this occasion he went down in a convincing manner which had me assaulting the air waves with the cry that a stretcher would surely be required to carry him to a waiting ambulance. However, the bold Davie quickly revived sufficiently to remonstrate in no uncertain terms with Mr Cook. At this point the referee forced his way between Cook and Wilson and produced his book to note the names of both players. The whistler's temper wasn't improved when Davie Wilson suddenly went into fits of laughter.

Later Wilson told me that the ridiculous side of the situation had dawned on him at the instant the referee arrived on the scene. There they were, three little men, glaring balefully at each other. 'Och ref, this is daft,' said Davie. 'There's no' five feet between the three of us.'

Drawing himself up to his full height, which required the merest effort on his part, the referee replied in the most dignified voice he could command in the circumstances: 'I happen to be 5ft 4.'

Discussing the thankless job of refereeing recently with a young man who has not long started on the long and difficult road which has to be negotiated successfully before the aspirant can hope to become a senior referee, I was disappointed to hear that attacks on referees are increasing in the lower levels of our game. There can be absolutely no excuse for this and very severe punishments must be meted out to the clubs concerned before this type of behaviour becomes the norm. Not that the offering of violence to refs is confined to the lower levels of the Scottish game.

Abroad it can be an even greater problem. Bobby Davidson, our World Cup representative in West Germany in 1974, recounted to me an incident which took place in Portugal which could have had severe repercussions. Bobby had given a decision against the home team among whose supporters were a number of patients from a local hospital. These were grouped right down at the retaining wall opposite the centre line.

As Davidson lectured the offending player, there was a loud roar from the crowd behind his back which alerted him to potential trouble. He spun round, only just in time to see one of the patients, a huge fellow who, despite the considerable handicap of having only one leg, had somehow managed to scramble over the wall. He had his crutch poised as a javelin and aimed at where the referee's back had been a second before. Luckily the noise of the crowd had saved Bobby from serious injury.

At home a less serious and indeed comical attack would have injured the referee's pride more than his person had it succeeded. Former official David Murdoch, of Bothwell, reaped little reward for his efforts in a game featuring Alloa Athletic and Dumbarton. The Alloa officials were apparently displeased at Mr Murdoch's handling of the game, and as the referee was dressing after the match the door opened and a missile hurtled

And It's All Over . . .

Alex. Totten points the way ahead for St. Johnstone. Alex played for Liverpool, Dundee, Dunfermline, Falkirk, Queen of the South and Alloa. He also managed Alloa, Falkirk, Rangers (Assist) and Dumbarton before taking over St. Johnstone. But the question remains, did he throw a mince pie at referee David Murdoch? Picture by Bob Bruce.

through the air, narrowly missing him. The missile on this occasion was less lethal than a crutch — although there are those who would claim only a little less lethal — it was a good old fashioned pie! The current St Johnstone manager and former Rangers assistant Manager Alex Totten, then in charge of Alloa, to this day refuses to tell me who hurled the offending pie.

Perhaps the body of opinion that suggests referees be paid danger money has a point after all. I might go further and suggest that it be paid generally and not for specific high-risk games. What, after all, could be less likely to provoke aggression between players, fans or referees than a five-a-side tournament organised by an amateur club? What indeed!

Glasgow's Kelvin Hall was the venue for the annual tournament run by Giffnock North AFC. As compère for the tournament, I urged the spectators always to decide which team they intended to shout for and thus ensure that the atmosphere was kept at a good level.

Who'd Be a Referee?

This exhortation was not necessary, of course, when the professional invitation tournament, run as a supplement to the competition, got under way. On one occasion Rangers fielded a five all of whom had played for Scotland, including that feared competitor, Tom Forsyth. However, far from getting things all their own way, the Ibrox five found themselves in opposition to a Hibs side led by an equally keen competitor in the bulky shape of Joe Harper.

Now in five-a-side football the space is confined and the ball is rarely out of play. Thus there is little time in which to cool tempers should they flare, which they sometimes do. Additionally, an innocent-looking tackle, judiciously launched, can send an opponent crashing into the retaining wall, an occurrence which can cause considerable pain to the victim. Nor should anyone be lulled into a false sense of security by the fact that the footwear is restricted to 'trainers.' The sole of a 'trainer,' aimed at a vulnerable spot, can be a painful and dangerous weapon.

It follows, therefore, when competition is keen, that the referee can have a more difficult job ensuring that the set of beer mugs or whatever the particular fives prize is, is won fairly, than he might have in trying to ensure that the European Cup reaches its rightful destination.

Tom Gray, now an SFA referee supervisor, was the unhappy controller of the five-a-side tournament of which I write. Inevitably, it transpired that Messrs Forsyth and Harper were unable to agree as to the legality of a tackle by the former on the latter. As referee Gray stepped in to pour oil on troubled waters, one or other of the feuding pair decided that arbitration would not bring about a satisfactory conclusion and threw the father and mother of right hooks. The punch didn't reach its desired target, and Tom Gray's handsome appearance belies the fact that he has two false teeth at the front of his mouth.

Besieged on all sides, the referee's lot is seldom a happy one. Considering the scant money they earn and the dog's abuse they take, I sometimes wonder why they do the job at all. Either they're a bunch of masochists or, more likely, like an awful lot of people on this planet they're hooked on a game that simultaneously unites and divides mankind. As the ultimate symbol of authority they provoke our spleen. And in Scotland I happen to believe that most of them do an almost impossible job well most of the time.

14

Scottish Football's Blackest Day

January 2, 1971 was the saddest day in the history of Scottish football, and the half-hearted report I broadcast for the BBC that evening was the most irrelevant that it has ever been my duty to do.

On that day Rangers played Celtic at Ibrox in the traditional Ne'erday fixture, but for once the result mattered naught. Celtic went ahead through Jimmy Johnstone near the end of the match and many disappointed Rangers fans began to make their way towards the exits at their end of the ground.

But with only seconds remaining Rangers' striker Colin Stein scored an equaliser. Hearing the roar that signalled the goal, many departing Rangers fans turned and rushed back up the fateful stairway 13 just as the referee blew the final whistle.

Thousands more turned in the opposite direction towards the exit and the meeting of both masses resulted in the greatest tragedy ever to hit the Scottish game. Many fans fell under the weight of the departing supporters and were crushed to death with those leaving the stadium unable to stop because of the weight of humanity behind.

When the horror was finally halted, sixty-six fans lay dead and many more were injured, a scenario that made anything that had happened in the match of no consequence whatsoever.

Like thousands of other spectators who had left by different exits, I was totally unaware of the catastrophe as I left the ground right on the final whistle. A car was waiting to whisk me back to the BBC studios to beat the expected traffic jams so that my voice report on the match would be transmitted in good time.

When I reached Broadcasting House the first person I met

was Peter Thomson. His first words were: 'What a terrible business at Ibrox.' I didn't know what he was talking about, but as the full dimensions of the tragedy began to unfold as the news filtered steadily into the BBC, another chilling possibility dawned on me.

My son Michael, then 18, had been at the match on that terracing. Oh God ... what if? I believe I mechanically recorded a minute's report detailing the bare facts of the game. Who cared anyway? By now news reporters were swarming all over Ibrox piecing together the horrific details of the biggest story in the long history of Scottish football. Among the volunteers helping to move the dead and injured were the respective managers, Willie Waddell of Rangers, and Jock Stein of Celtic.

I sat down to think of my family and my next move. I didn't want to 'phone Sheila and worry her unnecessarily in case she knew nothing about the accident. On the other hand I had to know about Michael. I swithered but by 6 o'clock I could wait no longer and picked up the 'phone and dialled my home number.

Thank God. Michael had just walked in the door safe and sound and, like my wife who hadn't been listening to radio or television, was also unaware of anything untoward. He had left the game by another exit. My relief was considerable. It was, as I've said, the blackest day in Scottish football.

Yet in the strange way that it does, disaster unites people where previously there has been division. The divided city of Glasgow was as one in mourning for the dead and bereaved.

For a time at any rate. But unfortunately not for all time.

15

The New Firm

If my early days of commentary were dominated by the wonderful achievements in Europe of the Old Firm of Celtic in Lisbon in 1967 and Rangers in Barcelona in 1972, my latter-day memories encompass the superb efforts of Scotland's New Firm of Aberdeen and Dundee United.

How I would dearly have loved to announce, in my final broadcast featuring a Scottish club in European competition, that Dundee United had beaten Gothenburg to win the UEFA Cup. That wasn't to be as it turned out, but more of the event and Jim McLean's 'Tangerine Terrors' later.

As coincidence had it, Dundee United's visit to Gothenburg in the first leg of the UEFA Final of 1987 was a retracing of the footsteps of the other half of the New Firm. Four years earlier had come the greatest moment of Aberdeen's eighty-year history. In the bedlam of Gothenburg's magnificent, if rain-soaked, Ullevi Stadium, the Dons had brushed aside the challenge of one of Europe's most famous sides, Real Madrid, to score a 2-1 victory and win the European Cupwinners Cup. Yet it had been a nail-biting experience for their 10,000 or so travelling supporters as well as the thousands more at home who watched the game on TV or listened on radio.

Our commentary team of David Begg, Murdoch McPherson and myself had barely got ourselves settled in our commentary cabin when Eric Black blasted the ball past the Real goalkeeper Augustin to put Aberdeen one goal up. Only seven minutes had gone and every Scot in the Ullevi Stadium swelled with pride and confidence. However, those who had watched the exploits of the great Real Madrid should have known better than to take victory for granted.

A penalty goal by Juanito after Jim Leighton had pulled

A meeting with a foreign colleague, Thomas Simson, the leading Swedish football commentator, before the first leg of the UEFA Cup final between Gothenburg and Dundee United in Sweden in 1987.

down Isidro saw the teams level at half time and, with the deadlock unbroken at full time the game moved into extra time. The weariness in the legs of the players was matched by the huskiness in the throats of the commentators, David Begg and myself.

But Aberdeen's triumph had only been delayed. With just three minutes left, that marvellous late starter on his career, Peter Weir, sent away Mark McGhee. Over came an inch-perfect cross and I almost leaped as high as John Hewitt, microphone and all, as the Aberdeen substitute, who had only been brought on for extra time, rose to head a superb winner.

Incredible scenes followed as manager Alex Ferguson and his assistant Archie Knox were carried shoulder high towards the delirious but well-behaved Scottish fans. The late Chris Anderson, the vice chairman of Aberdeen, whose early death was a sad loss to his beloved team and Scottish football, commented that night: 'This is certainly the greatest moment in our history but it is also one of the great moments in the history of Scottish football.' My friend Chris was right. The entire Aberdeen entourage of directors, management, players and fans were a credit to Scotland and their club and were fêted and highly praised by the town of Gothenburg and all with whom they came into contact.

'This is the greatest day of my life' was how the architect of that and many another Aberdeen triumph, my longstanding friend, manager Alex Ferguson, was to sum it up. Undoubtedly Ferguson's managerial skills will achieve many more successes on the football stage. But I doubt if any will prove sweeter.

I've known Fergie since he was a young player with Dunfermline Athletic, so you could say we're old friends. That hasn't prevented us from falling out.

Football managers can be almost paranoid about criticism. They take as an insult to themselves anything of a critical nature that is said about their teams. I suppose it's that way because of the nature of a job which puts them under so much personal stress.

And yet no one can go through a game, involved to such an extent as a radio commentator is, without giving an opinion. We always try to be strictly neutral, but if the commentator sees something happening that appears blatantly unfair it is the most natural thing in the world to comment upon it. Indeed it is a duty to do so.

My big fall out with Ferguson came after a Celtic-Aberdeen match at Parkhead, a fixture which in recent years has been keenly competitive, often highly controversial and just as often downright physical.

Paul McStay, Celtic's talented young midfield player, was booked for a foul on an Aberdeen player and I passed over to my summariser for a comment with the observation that it had been a bookable offence. The chap who was sharing the commentary with me replied: 'Yes, but Paul has taken a few knocks himself and I think he was just getting some of his own back.'

This got to Fergie's ears as a statement that I had made. He was furious about it. The next time I was working at Pittodrie I asked him in the foyer for his team before the kick off. He just glared at me and for reply said: 'You're like a lot of others in your business. You like to curry favour with the Old Firm.'

I asked him what I was supposed to have said and he replied: 'You know perfectly well what you said in your commentary at Parkhead' and turned on his heel and walked away.

This rankled with me and I was genuinely baffled by his reaction. I later went to my producer, Charles Runcie, and asked him if he could think of anything I had said during commentary that would have upset Fergie. Charles was good enough to play the entire tape of the broadcast back and concluded: 'I couldn't find anything at all that you said, David. The only thing that may have ruffled him was the summariser's comment that McStay had been taking a few knocks himself before he was booked.'

That was enough for me. Soon afterwards Aberdeen were playing Hearts at Tynecastle and, filled with righteous indignation, I made straight for the visitors' dressingroom when I arrived at the ground and knocked firmly on the door.

It was opened by Fergie. Looking straight through me he said: 'What do you want?' I stared back at him and said: 'I just want to say to you that you were wrong in assuming that I had said anything detrimental to Aberdeen during the Celtic match. I've had the tape played back to prove it.' He didn't reply, simply walked inside and closed the dressingroom door.

But my point had apparently gone home. The following Wednesday I travelled with Aberdeen for a European tie and Fergie was his old pleasant self again, as if nothing had happened. But then I'd seen it all before, starting many years previously with Jock Stein.

It seems part of the very ingredients that make such men good managers: their restless energy and quick-tempered reactions can also make them very difficult to deal with at times.

As far as the east of Scotland is concerned, there is also a bit of a chip on a few collective shoulders over what they discern, quite wrongly in my view, as a bias in favour of the two big Glasgow clubs by the media in the west.

The facts are that the bulk of the newspapers have their headquarters in the west, the main BBC and Scottish Television studios are there and radio, too, so there may at times be a good financial reason for not travelling, say, to Aberdeen if there is an equally or even more meaningful game in Glasgow.

But there is no justifiable complaint in how east-coast teams are reported, and I think the New Firm of Aberdeen and Dundee United would agree that their recent exploits have received fair and proportionate coverage. Nor has the recent resurgence of Hearts in Edinburgh been ignored by the 'western' press.

As far as I am concerned personally, a large proportion of my more enjoyable assignments have been at places like Pittodrie, Tannadice, Tynecastle, Easter Road and so on.

It is true that the Old Firm of Rangers and Celtic attract massive doses of unending publicity, both good and bad. It is what managers regard as the bad publicity that creates extra pressures on them, and this is something that no east-coast club, however successful, has to contend with.

My good friend, the late Jimmy Sanderson, a highly experienced journalist and broadcaster, touched on the matter in a very concise way at the time both Ferguson and Jim McLean were being tipped as contenders for the vacant Rangers management job after John Greig had left. Said Jimmy: 'They've got a lot to think of before they come down here. In their own parish they've got the press going for them. In Glasgow they'll find things a lot different and they'll be judged more harshly by the media.'

I wouldn't doubt that Ferguson has found this to be the case in Manchester. And Graeme Souness, for all his success at Rangers, hasn't had a totally sympathetic press.

But to continue with the other half of the New Firm.

Four years on and Jim McLean, Alex Ferguson's friend and management rival, was to come so close to savouring

Smiling in the rain with Aberdeen and Scotland's last line of defence ... Jim Leighton, Willie Miller and the joker in the pack, big Alex McLeish.

European success, this time in the UEFA Cup, in the same Ullevi Stadium in Gothenburg. It looked as if 1987 would be the year when the man who made a provincial Scottish club into one to be respected and feared, not only in Scotland but in Europe, would receive the kind of deserved reward that had eluded him for so long.

On their way to the UEFA Cup final Dundee United had disposed of such European notables as Hajduk Split of Yugoslavia, and the multi-millionaires of Barcelona. Indeed United's wins over the Spaniards, first at Tannadice on March 4th and again in the fabulous Camp Nou Stadium, will rank among their best in Europe. I well recall that second-leg tie.

United had travelled to Barcelona leading by the only goal scored at Tannadice by young Kevin Gallacher with a cross from the right which completely deceived goalkeeper Zubizarreta with less than two minutes played. But if United had struck early in the first-leg tie, they left it late in Barcelona.

Before a roaring 42,000 crowd, the famous Spaniards

scored through Caldere just before half time to make the tie equal on aggregate at 1-1. Ashamed as I am to admit it and although I attempted to project confidence during my broadcast, I honestly felt that United were on the way out.

Now it so happened that seated beside me on the plane to Barcelona was a charming lady by the name of Mrs Clark, whose son John, a broth of a young man, had other ideas about United's exit from the tournament.

John had left his wife in a Dundee hospital where she was due to become a mother, and no sooner had I announced this titbit of information to the listeners than John had me bringing his name to the attention of the audience again, this time as he crashed an unsaveable header against the underside of the crossbar and into the Barcelona net. Now it was 2-1 to United on aggregate with only four minutes left. The Camp Nou Stadium was stunned. Three minutes later it was shattered as Ian Ferguson met a Paul Sturrock chip with his head and United were through to the semi final.

And Borussia Moenchengladbach fared no better in the semi. They survived the trip to a rainsodden Tannadice with a no-scoring draw, but met with a solid 2-0 defeat in the Bokelberg Stadium. So for the Tangerine Terrors it was on to Gothenburg on the 6th of May with the hope of becoming the first Scottish team to win the UEFA Cup. These hopes were high indeed.

Had they succeeded I would have led the applause because, in my experience, there is no friendlier club in the country and none more worthy of success at the highest level.

I think it is worth mentioning here that during United's European campaign of 1987 I detected a perceptible change in manager Jim McLean. Jim has consistently projected the image of a rather dour, humourless person. The fact is that he is a perfectionist as far as football is concerned and is, therefore, more likely to be displeased than jubilant in the course of a long hard season. But it was a more relaxed Jim McLean who led United in their UEFA campaign.

I can well remember at the press conference for the British and European media before the first leg of the final in the

'Good to see you back in Scotland.' A word of welcome to 'Champagne' Charlie Nicholas. Charlie was acclaimed the best David Francey mimic in the Scottish International Squad.

Ullevi Stadium, Jim being asked if he had chosen his team for the game. 'No, I've still to ask Doris [his wife] about it,' he joked.

Alas, neither the relaxed Jim McLean nor two fine performances by United were sufficient to realise their cherished dream of bringing the UEFA Cup to Tannadice. A header by Petterson gave Gothenburg a single-goal advantage when the teams lined up for the second leg at Tannadice.

Defeated United may have been. They must also have suffered the biggest disappointment in their history, but their stature in European football had been vastly increased that night.

As if in recognition of that, the fans at Tannadice boosted immeasurably the image of Dundee United and Scottish football by the marvellous ovations they gave not only their own team in defeat but Gothenburg, the side that had deprived them of their finest hour. It was an example of sportsmanship, rarely seen in any modern sport and all the more praiseworthy when one recalls that only four days earlier those same fans had watched their heroes lose the Scottish Cup Final to St Mirren although starting favourites to win the tie.

So my final thoughts on Dundee United are of a team aspiring to bring all that is best in football to a game which has thrived over a century, in part by producing managerial geniuses like Jim McLean. United may never achieve the success their high standards deserve but I will always remember that they provided material for some of the most exciting broadcasts of my career, and I shall remember, too, the welcoming, friendly atmosphere of Tannadice.

16

The Principals

If you were to ask a football fan to name the best players he had ever seen, he would, no doubt, rhyme off the eleven wearing, or who had worn, his team's colours, plus, probably, the substitutes.

I remember presenting a league winner's medal at a function in Glasgow to a young man heavily swathed in green and white. 'I can see who you support,' I said. Having shaken hands with about 150 young men already that evening, I was running out of original material. He wasn't! 'Oh, no,' he replied. 'I'm not a one man team. I support two, Celtic and Celtic Reserves.'

However, when you have travelled the world watching the game's top exponents over three decades, such an embarrassment of riches is involved that pinpoint selection becomes impossible.

One great danger in an exercise of this nature, if undertaken, is to search for the exotic names at the expense of the John Greigs, Billy McNeills, Willie Millers, Paul Hegartys and so on. Somehow, with a name like Eusebio or Pele or Jairzinho or Di Stefano one feels you should be a better player. I could be falling into that trap. Certainly one of the greatest players I have ever seen was the great Eusebio, the fabulous Black Panther of Benfica and Portugal. Not only was he a player of immense grace, litheness and talent, he was also one of the most charming men I have met in all my years of globe-trotting.

I well remember the occasion of an international between Portugal and Scotland in Lisbon in 1978. I introduced myself to him as the players were standing around in the main foyer area outside the dressingrooms in the National Stadium an hour or so before the kick off.

He spoke marvellous English and we had quite a

conversation. Without prompting he said: 'Please send my kind regards over the air to the people of Scotland. I have always enjoyed my visits to your country very much.'

I told him that the feelings of the Scottish football supporters for him and his talent were mutual and that I would indeed pass on his good wishes.

Just then, Martin Buchan, the Manchester United and Scotland defender, walked past. I asked Martin how he fancied the job of marking the great Black Panther. 'He's only got two legs the same as anyone else,' replied the laconic Buchan. Oh really? How I wish more British players had had the talent of Eusebio. The result, in that match incidentally, was a narrow 1-0 win for Portugal.

One British player whose talents were in the same league as Eusebio's was George Best. I recall him almost beating Scotland single-handed in a Home International Championship match at Windsor Park in Belfast in 1971, and you could count on the fingers of one hand the number of players in the world let alone a province the size of Northern Ireland who had the sheer genius to have the entire opposition on tenterhooks.

Denis Law, a team-mate and contemporary of Best's at Old Trafford, was possibly the outstanding Scot of his generation as Kenny Dalglish would be of the next. Denis was a great penalty box player, the sharpest thing on two feet, and it has been a great privilege to get to know him better in his latter-day role as a broadcaster with whom I have worked on many occasions in the commentary box.

Without hesitation, though, I would say that the finest collection of club players I have seen on the same park at the same time was when I stood on the terracing at Hampden Park on the 18th of May, 1960, as just one of a fascinated crowd of 135,000 to watch the mighty Real Madrid beat Eintracht Frankfurt 7-3 in one of the greatest European Cup Finals ever played.

Thousands of the fans had gone to Hampden that night hoping to see the West German champions get their comeuppance. After all, Eintracht had had the temerity to beat Glasgow Rangers in the semi final by an embarrassing

The Principals

aggregate of 12-4. But those frustrated Rangers fans stood on long after the final whistle to cheer Spaniard and German alike, with some extra applause for the magical Real side which read:

Dominguez; Marquitos, Pachin; Vidal, Santamaria, Zarraga; Canario, Del Sol, Di Stefano, Puskas, Ghento.

Real's goals were shared by Di Stefano, who got three, and Puskas, who got the other four. It was the Spaniards' fifth European Cup win in a row as they totally dominated the early years of the competition. Every player was a star in his own right. Real had two formal wingers, Canario on the right and Ghento on the left. Del Sol was an orthodox inside right with the Hungarian 'Galloping Major' Ferenc Puskas at deep inside left.

Di Stefano was the real eye opener, though. Wearing the number nine, he should have operated in those days as the centre forward or in today's terms the main striker.

Not Di Stefano. One minute this brilliant Argentinian was receiving an under-arm throw from Dominguez on his own 18-yard line, next he was thundering the ball into the Eintracht net from 20 yards out.

And how the crowd gasped when Puskas fired an almighty drive after Canario or Ghento had torn the German defence apart.

I remember two comments made that night by a little Glasgow man standing beside me with the spontaneous humour of the terracing, a thing I missed a lot in my later isolation in the commentary box. This fellow wasn't concealing his loyalties although he was close to being concealed himself in the blue and white muffler and blue bunnet he wore. His first comment to me came late in the game after Ghento had taken on four players, left them all for dead, and, without breaking stride, hit a cross-shot which rattled the bar on its way over. 'He'll be drapped next week for missin' that wan,' quoth the terracing philosopher.

Again, when the little winger had opened up the Eintracht defence and let Puskas in to score: 'Ah've been thinkin, the 'Gers should sell Ibrox and buy that wee yin.'

But how can you compare individual players? Would anyone

doubt that little 5ft 3in Jimmy Johnstone was a world-class player? So, too, Dalglish but he and 'Jinky' were essentially different types of player.

Jim Baxter and Ian McMillan were the heroes of Ibrox in the early '60s, yet Ian has told me more than once that without big Harry Davis, the magic of Baxter and McMillan would have been seen a great deal less. 'You've got to get the ball before you can use it,' said Ian. 'Big Harry got the ball for us and then we used it.'

If I am reluctant to try to compare the talents of one player with another, it is largely because I have been privileged to watch so many highly talented performers and to select one would mean omitting others.

Believe me, to have the chance to do something one enjoys and be paid for it is indeed one of life's great privileges.

17

The Future

I

The Club Scene – Exciting or Worrying?

It could be argued that I have probably left the Scottish football scene at one of its most exciting periods. And perhaps that possibility was underlined most heavily by a supporter of Greenock Morton to whom I talked just before the 1986/7 season started. My good friends at Greenock will pardon me,

Francey, flanked by leaders of the Rangers revolution, Ibrox player-manager Graeme Souness and assistant Walter Smith. Picture courtesy Alan Ewing.

which normally enjoys football of world class. The excitement of my friend was, therefore, understandable. He said, almost breathlessly, 'You know, Davie, I can hardly believe it. Next season I'll go along to Cappielow as usual, but I'll be able to see Souness, Butcher, Woods, Roberts, Nichol all on the park at the same time. It'll be like watching our boys taking on an international team.'

He was, of course, referring to the Rangers influx of world-class stars. Now he could add Avi Cohen, Trevor Francis, Ray Wilkins, Mark Walters and Ian Ferguson. He can also delight in watching Celtic's Frank McAvennie, Mick McCarthy and Chris Morris. He can see Scotland's Andy Goram in the Hibernian goalkeeping jersey, and Aberdeen's Peter Nicholas, Keith Edwards and Charlie Nicholas, all of whom have taken a one-way ticket North of the Border. For this influx of fabulous football talent I give full marks to the Board of Glasgow Rangers. What I do not understand is how it took so long for the decision to be made to spend big. Big-name stars and a winning Rangers side were always going to produce capacity crowds, not only at Ibrox, but as has been proved with Rangers' massive travelling support, at every ground they visit. I said years ago that this could happen. Lawrence Marlborough and David Holmes have made it happen. I applaud their foresight and courage.

Yet, unfortunately, the influx of this footballing talent to Scotland has brought its problems. Bookings, orderings off and eventually police prosecution have put the livelihoods of those same superstars in jeopardy. Investigation into the circumstances of the troubles must be deep and thorough. The question must be asked, 'Why is it that Graeme Souness can play in arguably Europe's toughest school, Italy, and in England without earning the reputation that he has earned after a relatively short time in Scotland?' If Souness alone were the only culprit one could conclude that he was entirely to blame for what has been happening, but Terry Butcher, Chris Woods, Graham Roberts, Frank McAvennie and Mick McCarthy have all been on the receiving end of the red card since they moved North of the Border. Now the law has moved in in what I

The Future

consider a most serious precedent. What constitutes a charge of actions likely to cause a breach of the peace? Is a footballer liable to be arrested for tripping an opponent as he looks likely to score? That could surely cause a riot in the crowd. What about the boxer who butts an opponent? It happens in nearly every fight and could cause trouble amongst the spectators. Do the police step in, stop the fight and cart the offender off to jail? One could go on postulating situations which could arise. Football is a game for athletes. It is a contact sport. To reach the top a player has to be fit, strong and skilful. Jock Wallace, whom I admired tremendously as a manager and as a person, told me once when I was trying to commiserate with him over the injury in training to one of his star players at Ibrox: 'I told him it was his own fault. He should have had his leg out of the way.'

Remember that world class Dutchman, Johan Cruyff? It was my pleasure and, indeed, delight, to watch that master in action on many occasions. Cruyff, if heavily tackled – and a player of his class is always open to it – didn't spend the following minutes rolling about in supposed agony. He was on his feet chasing the ball before the offending defender had had time to think of an excuse for the benefit of the referee. I only wish that here in Scotland players would follow that example. I know from personal experience the pain of a twisted knee or studs drawn down the calf muscles, but every footballer knows that he must be prepared to face up to foul or even dangerous play. As a more famous name than mine is accredited with saying, 'If you can't stand the heat, get out of the kitchen.'

So I put forward this plea to the Scottish Football Association, The Scottish Football League, referees, clubs, players, and perhaps, above all, the custodians of the Law. Think very carefully about what is happening to our beloved game in Scotland. We have greater talent and more of it here today than we have ever had. This must surely be to the benefit of everyone in the game and to the vast and ever-growing army of followers throughout our nation. You face a fragile and difficult situation. Diplomacy, investigative skills and common sense are required to resolve it. My knowledge of the current

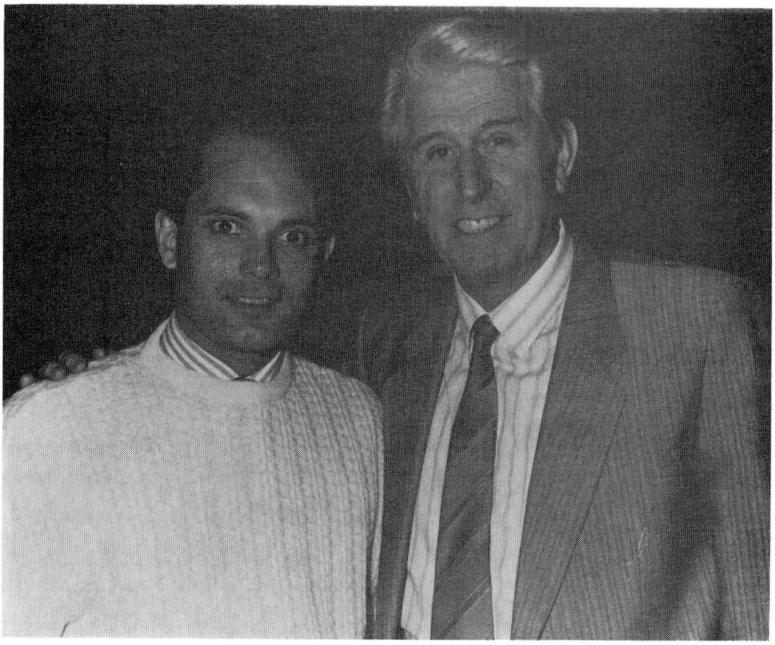

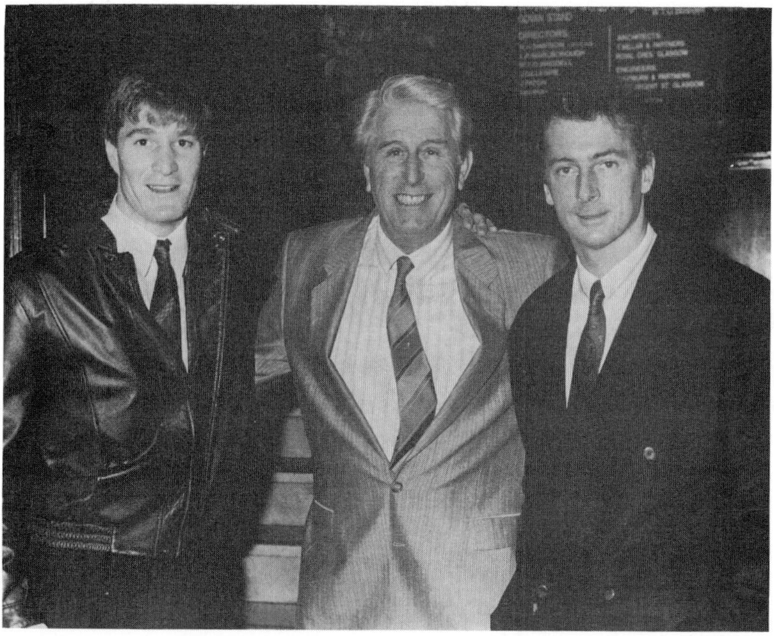

Francey in the middle of the English invasion of Ibrox. Richard Gough shows a natty line in leatherwear, Trevor Francis is slightly more formal, Ray Wilkins prefers knitwear, and Graham Roberts sports a business suit as he autographs a ball. Pictures courtesy Alan Ewing.

administrators and the players gives me great hope that it will work out well. So be it.

II

Andy and Craig – The Jordanhill Mafia

'The Jordanhill mafia's in charge' was the opinion of many in the game when educationalists Andy Roxburgh and Craig Brown were appointed Chief and Assistant International Coaches by the S.F.A. 'Subutteo Managers' was another title given to the pair in anticipation of the blackboard tactics. Well, let me be quite frank about it: I applauded the appointments of Roxburgh and Brown and I am confident that, given reasonable time, they will do an excellent job for Scotland.

The main criticism levelled at the two by certain influential sections of the media was their lack of managerial experience

At the seat of power. On the steps of the Scottish Football Association Headquarters flanked by Secretary Ernie Walker, National Coach Andy Roxburgh and his assistant Craig Brown on Ernie Walker's right. Picture Alan Ewing.

at club level. True, Craig Brown was assistant manager at Motherwell for a time and manager of Clyde. However, neither Roxburgh nor Brown was a player or manager of top status.

My reaction to such criticism is the same as that of those who appointed them – 'So what?' I have been in the business

The Future

world long enough to know that the best plumber in the squad does not necessarily make the best foreman. The skilful accountant who shines in his profession does not always make the best business manager. The football business is full of examples of fine players who failed as managers, and equally there are examples of successful club managers who made no impact on the international scene. I believe at international level a coach is required who can blend good players into a team. That, as I've said earlier, was Willie Ormond's theory. 'They are all good players,' the wee man told me. 'If they weren't they wouldn't be playing for top teams in Scotland, England, Ireland, Wales and others with the elite of Europe. So anyone can pick eleven good players. The trick is to blend them into a team!'

As I write this, it looks as though the duo of nice guys, Andy Roxburgh and Craig Brown, are getting their act and Scotland's together successfully.

I wish them well.

18
And It's All Over! . . .

And so, if I may be permitted a final Franceyism — there goes the final whistle.

Thirty-five years may not be a lifetime in the 'three score years and ten' of the biblical assessment of average human existence, but in the difficult, stressful business of live spontaneous broadcasting, however much one enjoys the subject of one's broadcasts, it is a lifetime. So in this period of retrospection, I am grateful to have been given down the years the health, the strength and the ability, as well as the support of so many friends and associates in the business. Clearly I cannot name them all and indeed, in the unique world of broadcasting one may never come face to face with, or hear the name of, a producer, engineer or secretary without whose efforts the Francey voice from Budapest, or Rio de Janeiro or Lisbon or Firhill would not have been heard.

So let me name a representative few, with the unnamed, I hope, aware of and sharing in my gratitude.

I have spoken elsewhere about the late Peter Thomson, without whom the Francey Voice of Football might never have grown beyond a cherished dream. Peter was followed as Head of Sport by a handsome young Irishman whose acquaintance I had made in his role of producer. Then he would accompany the Irish commentator who would share commentary with me when our countries met. His name is Malcolm Kellard and his help and support, especially in far-off places like Argentina, will always be remembered.

Then there was the late Murdoch McPherson, Church of Scotland minister, producer and broadcaster, responsible for updating the 'Sportsound' programme by introducing the instant news flashes from around the sporting scene as soon

Welcome home Frank. David congratulates Frank McAvennie on the completion of his £750,000 transfer from West Ham which made him Celtic's most expensive player. Picture courtesy John Cullen and Andy Feeney.

as they happened. A formidable man with a talk-back facility which meant that during commentary he could speak to the commentator from the studio whilst that poor chap (usually myself) could not reply without the world and his neighbour listening in.

Many and heated were the post mortems on why, for example, a direction from the studio nerve centre to leave the commentary momentarily and switch to, say, Gerry Davis at Pittodrie as Aberdeen had just scored, had not been acted upon. 'Because,' would come my equally heated rejoinder, 'with Celtic and Rangers standing at one goal each and Rangers threatening the Celtic goal for the winner, were the millions of listeners throughout the world really more interested to know at that very second that Aberdeen had scored a sixth goal against whoever?'

Of course such judgements were very fine indeed and I can honestly never remember an occasion, when we had deliberately switched away from the commentary game, that we missed a goal by so doing. This calls for a high standard of team work between producer and commentator, and I believe Murdoch and I achieved this just as we achieved a solid and lasting friendship. Despite the great sadness I felt at his untimely death at the age of only 52, I felt honoured to be invited by the BBC to broadcast an obituary of Murdoch. I hope I did him justice.

Lest this final chapter take more words than the rest of the book, let me confine myself now to names. Such as my early day television producers Bill Malcolm and Charles Munro, the studio managers and audio engineers without whom no sound would be heard, Iris, Eric, Neal, Dave, Max, among many, many more. And where would we be without the secretaries, the Isobels, Normas, Lindas, producers such as Charles Runcie and Rob Hastie, both now guiding the interests of Radio 2 sport, and so on ...

Nor have I even mentioned, as yet, the presenters past and present, like Roy Small, Brian Marjoribanks and Tom Ferrie, long-serving reporters in the mould of Bob Seith and Gordon Smith and Scottish commentators who have shared the commentary cabin with me such as Radio Clyde's Gerry McNee.

And outside Scotland, I recall with gratitude those two fine presenters who made me feel at ease, particularly during my early days of broadcasting, the late Eamonn Andrews and BBC World Service's Paddy Feeney.

For past encouragement and a champagne send off may I also thank BBC Scotland Controller Pat Chalmers.

A final little anecdote. Some five years before I decided to hang up my microphone I received a most courteous letter, postmarked Aberdeen, from a young man, aged 14, telling me that he would like to be a football commentator and asking me for my advice.

How much that advice helped I'll never know. But I'm prepared to say that even without it the young man would still have achieved his ambition.

It is therefore with particular pleasure that I close this book knowing that Radio Scotland's number one commentary position is in the capable hands and voice of that same young man, Derek Rae. May he enjoy the happy and fulfilling career it has been my good fortune to experience.

And ... it's all over!

Three generations. A happy family picture showing Sheila and David with son Michael, his wife Dorothy, grandchildren Donna and Alan (standing) and namesake David relaxing at the front of the group. Picture Alan Ewing.

Index

Luis Agnolin (Italy), 2
Willie Allan, 62
Chris Anderson, 94, 95
Eamonn Andrews, 117
Ian Archer, 35, 36, 80

Joe Baker, 24
Jim Baxter, 20, 106
David Begg, 74, 93, 94
George Best, 104
Eric Black, 93
Gordon Blair, 31
John Blair, 37, 38, 80
Billy Bremner, 55, 56, 60, 61
Bobby Brown, 54
Craig Brown 2, 80, 111, 112, 113
Jock Brown 80
Martin Buchan, 69, 104
Terry Butcher, 108
BBC Engineers and Secretaries, 117

Eric Caldow, 7
Andy Cameron, 66
Canario (Real Madrid), 105
Carlos (Brazil), 1
Pat Chalmers, 117
Stevie Chalmers, 76
John Clark, 99
David Coleman, 34, 78, 79, 80
Avi Cohen, 108
Alfie Conn, 57
Jim Cook, 85, 86
Davie Cooper, 41
Andy Cowan-Martin, 22, 23
Johan Cruyff (Holland), 109
Cubillas (Peru), 67
John Cushley, 46

Kenny Dalglish, 35, 55, 104, 106
Bobby Davidson, 87
George Davidson, 23
Gerry Davis, 116
Harry Davis, 106
Del Sol (Real Madrid), 105
Di Stefano (Real Madrid), 103, 105
Arthur Dixon, 9, 15
Tommy Docherty, 54, 55
Dominguez (Real Madrid), 105
Willie Donachie, 55
Robert Dunnet, 23

Keith Edwards, 108
Eusebio (Portugal), 20, 103, 104

Paddy Feeney, 117
Alex Ferguson, 94, 95, 96, 97
Ian Ferguson, 99, 108
Tam Ferguson, 21, 25
Tom Ferrie, 117
Tom Forsyth, 89
Trevor Francis, 108

Kevin Gallacher, 98
Willie Gardner, 5
Garincha (Real Madrid), 2
Archie Gemmell, 70
Geraldao (Brazil), 2
Ghento (Real Madrid), 105
Giffnock North AFC, 88
Andy Goram, 108
Arthur Graham, 56
Tom Gray, 89
Jimmy Greaves, 20
John Greig, 20, 34, 80, 97, 103,
Rankin Grimshaw, 58

Willie Harkness, 67
Joe Harper, 56, 89
Rob Hastie, 117
David Hay, 55
Paul Hegarty, 103
Allan Herron, 80
John Hewitt, 94
Tony Higgins, 31
David Holmes, 108
Jim Holton, 62

Colin Jackson, 55
Jairzinho (Brazil), 103
Jaunterino (Cuba), 34
Willie Johnston, 68, 69
Bobby Johnstone, 52
Jimmy Johnstone, 20, 43, 46, 55,
    106, 56, 91
Peter Jones, 30
Joe Jordan, 53, 55, 59, 61, 66
Juanito (Real Madrid), 93

Kasadi (Zaire), 59, 60, 61
Malcolm Kellard, 74, 115
Stewart Kennedy, 67
Archie Knox, 94

Denis Law, 20, 55, 74, 104
Jim Leighton, 93
Peter Lorimer, 55, 59

Frank McAvennie, 108
Mick McCarthy, 108
Willie McCartney, 52
Brian McClair, 3
Pat McCluskey, 56
Ally McCoist, 4
Phil McEntee, 80
Mark McGhee, 94
Danny McGrain, 55
Jim McLean, 93, 97, 99, 100, 101
Alex McLeish, 4
Hugh Dan McLennan, 84
Ally MacLeod, 54, 65, 66, 67, 72
Murdo MacLeod, 3
Ian McMillan, 26, 106
Gerry McNee, 117
Billy McNeill, 46, 103
Archie McPherson, 25
Murdoch McPherson, 83, 93, 115, 117
Paul McStay, 95, 96
Bill Malcolm, 117
Brian Marjoribanks, 117
Lawrence Marlborough, 108
Marquitos (Real Madrid), 105
John Martis, 24
Don Masson, 68, 69
Stanley Matthews, 20
Willie Miller, 3, 103
Mirandinha (Brazil), 2
Brian Moore, 75, 76
Chris Morris, 108
Don Morrison, 20
Muller (Brazil), 2
Munante (Peru), 67, 68
Charles Munro, 117
Luella & Margaret Munro, 20
David Murdoch, 87

Jimmy Nichol, 108
Charlie Nicholas, 3, 108
Peter Nicholas, 108

Willie Ormond, 65, 113

Pachin (Real Madrid), 105
Ian Paul, 80
Pele (Brazil), 2, 21, 103

Petterson (Gothenburg), 100
Puskas (Real Madrid), 105
Derek Rae, 118
Lawrie Reilly, 52
Liz Rennie, 20
Johnny Rep (Holland), 70
Jim Reynolds, 80
Ricardo (Brazil), 2
Bruce Rioch, 69
Rivelino (Brazil), 2
Graham Roberts, 108
Ken Robertson, 80
Alan Rough, 70
Andy Roxburgh, 2, 55, 111, 112, 113
Charles Runcie, 96, 117

Santamaria (Real Madrid), 105
Jimmy Sanderson, 97
Bob Seith, 117
George Slater, 84
Roy Small, 117
Dave Smith, 43
Gordon Smith, 52, 117
Graeme Souness, 97, 108
Colin Stein, 91
Jock Stein, 38, 41-50, 54, 57, 58, 62, 72, 92, 96
Paul Sturrock, 99

Peter Thomson, 17, 19, 23, 25, 26, 115
Alex Totten, 88
Eddie Turnbull, 52

Vidal (Real Madrid), 105

Willie Waddell, 92
Ernie Walker, 2
Jock Wallace, 109
Mark Walters, 108
Peter Weir, 94
Tom Wharton, 85
Ray Wilkins, 108
David Will, 2
Davie Wilson, 85, 86
Kenneth Wolstenholme, 76
Chris Woods, 108

Willie Young, 56

Zarraga (Real Madrid), 105
Zico (Brazil), 2
Zubizarreta (Barcelona), 98